TOP DAWGS

THE GEORGIA REMARKABLE ROAD to the NATIONAL CHAMPIONSHIP

SPECIAL COMMEMORATIVE BOOK

The Atlanta
Journal-Constitution

A COX ENTERPRISES COMPANY

Donna B. Hall, Publisher
Bala Sundaramoorthy, Vice President and General Manager
Kevin G. Riley, Editor
Mark A. Waligore, Managing Editor
Shawn McIntosh, Managing Editor
Leroy Chapman Jr., Managing Editor
Zachary McGhee, Senior Director, Digital Audience Experience
Chris Vivlamore, Sports Editor
Sandra Brown, Visuals Editor
Leo Willingham, Book Editor
Steve Hummer, Mark Bradley, Michael Cunningham, Chip Towers, Hyosub Shin, Curtis Compton,
Bob Andres, Stephen B. Morton, Jeff Sentell, Jason Getz, B.J. Sweeney, Connor Riley, Brandon Adams,
Barbara Vivlamore, Contributors

This book is available in quantity at special discounts for your group or organization.
For further information, contact:

Triumph Books LLC
814 North Franklin Street
Chicago, Illinois 60610
Phone: (312) 337-0747
www.triumphbooks.com

Printed in U.S.A.
Hardcover ISBN: 978-1-63727-135-3
Paperback ISBN: 978-1-63727-080-6

Content packaged by Mojo Media, Inc.
Joe Funk: Editor
Jason Hinman: Creative Director

Front cover photo by Curtis Compton/The Atlanta Journal-Constitution
Back cover photo by Hyosub Shin/The Atlanta Journal-Constitution

Curtis Compton/The Atlanta Journal-Constitution

CONTENTS

Foreword

By Loran Smith

If you subscribe to a pragmatic and egalitarian view, all of those involved with organizing, managing and playing the game of college football are No. 1. This grand old game has brought much honor and opportunity – to say nothing of an embarrassment of riches – to college campuses across the country.

While Georgia players are being fitted for championship rings, the rest of the nation, a large segment of it for sure, is preparing for the start of the 2022 season. They can't wait for fall practice, game day, tailgating, becoming cheerleaders with team logos on their rosy cheeks, the booming of the bass drums and the thrill of victory. To be the playoff champions of college football is the greatest thing since the Notre Dame box formation.

America, the land of the spread formation, stratospheric coaching salaries, treasured tailgate parking passes and homecoming kings and queens, just can't get enough of college football.

What all devoted fans most want is that no-name 26.5-inch, 35-pound, oblong, 24 karat gold, bronze and stainless-steel trophy that establishes from the Atlantic to the Pacific that your team is the champion of the college football world. Georgia now owns that trophy.

While the four-team format to decide the national champion is up for further review, in Athens and much of our Empire State of the South, no one could care less about that for the moment. The Bulldog faithful can point their right index finger to the heavens and proclaim they are No. 1 without any disclaimers.

There is nothing like sport to take an amalgamation of kids from the small towns of an agribusiness state and its metropolitan districts, along with a few from locales outside the state's borders. Take the big man Jordan Davis from Charlotte; the chairman of the running back committee Zamir White of Laurinburg, N.C.; a kid from Calabasas, Jermaine Burton, who likes to catch the ball, just like the walk-on kid, Ladd McConkey, who hails from the Blue Ridge Mountains of Chatsworth.

Then there are Nakobe Dean (Butkus Award Winner, 3.5 GPA student in engineering and good works célèbre in the community) from Horn Lake, Mississippi, just across Tom Sawyer's mighty river at Memphis; James Cook, the 5-foot-11 running back from Miami, who showed the home folks in the Orange Bowl that he belongs in the NFL, just like his brother; Big "O" Darnell Washington, the soft-spoken tight end from Las Vegas; and Brock Bowers, the other tight end from Napa, California, the greatest freshman in these United States.

It takes a village to win a championship, and in 2021 which segued into 2022, Georgia's village had personnel tentacles which stretched across the country, all united under the "G," designed more than four decades ago by a former assistant coach's wife.

The most heartwarming story is that of the beloved and castigated quarterback, who was underrated by the fans, but top rated in the locker room. Stetson Bennett, who can knock down a couple of quail on a covey rise or hook a five-pound bass on a South Georgia pond with the best of outdoorsmen, took all the slings and arrows – even from rabid Bulldog aficionados – and is now one of five Red and Black clad quarterbacks to win a national championship.

He is the toast of the state. He can thumb his nose at his critics, but he won't. He loves his university, he loves

his state and he loves his teammates. He is now Mr. Big Bull, but he won't act like it. Everybody can pull up a chair to his championship table and sup with him.

Let the celebration now gain momentum in Athens, Atlanta, Norcross (Jake Camarda), Milledgeville (Javon Bullard), Carrollton (Chaz Chambliss), Suwanee (Warren Ericson and Payne Walker), Gainesville (Dan Jackson), Fort Valley (Kearis Jackson), Brunswick (Warren McClendon), Cochran (Amarius Mims), St. Simons (Jack Podlesny), Powder Springs (Julian Rochester), Ellenwood (Justin Shaffer), Savannah (Nolan Smith), Cordele (Quay Walker), Thomaston (Travon Walker) and Decatur (Devonte Wyatt) among many places.

And a word about their indefatigable leader:

His surname defines him. In his personality makeup there is fire, energy, penultimate passion, raw-edged competitiveness and eternal drive. Kirby is a very SMART coach, and it shows.

These Dawgs had leadership from coaches to walk-on players. Most of all, the senior leadership was nonpareil. These Dawgs had talent. These Dawgs had verve. These Dawgs had muscle. These Dawgs had brotherly love. These Dawgs could hunt … with the best.

Let the Chapel Bell ring.

— **Loran Smith**
University of Georgia Athletics Historian

Introduction

By Steve Hummer

Go back to that December day in 2015 when Kirby Smart first gripped a podium as Georgia's head coach. The former Bulldogs safety, All-Conference in the late '90s, despite his constant claim of, "I wouldn't have signed me," had come home after accepting a single mission:

Take the Bulldogs on that final climb to the summit. Shake them from the comfortable base camp of being reliably good and haul them to that peak where only champions breathe the rarest air.

Those who scale mountains call the final exhausting obstacle of Everest the Hillary Step. Those who follow Georgia football would come to call that same sort of challenge Alabama.

How do you do it, how do you construct a program capable of not only consistently competing for a national title, but also winning one of the danged things, Smart was asked during his introductory press conference.

It had been so very long for Georgia; 1980's big-thighed Herschel Walker run to a championship being the property of some greatest generation of Bulldog was almost mythical 40-some years later.

"I think first and foremost these players at the University of Georgia have to believe in themselves," Smart answered. "We've got to do a good job of instilling them with that as a staff.

"There are good players here; we've got to do a good job with them. We've got to improve the depth. We've got to improve the quality of the depth throughout the team. Both offensive and defensive lines, skill areas, there is no area here that doesn't need improvement and depth. But that can be done. And I think it will be done."

Mission Accomplished. The belief, the growth, the glory, the whole megillah.

They have planted that big "G" flag at the roof of their world, which happened to be Indianapolis in this case. Yes, finally, the Bulldogs won another championship, and did it in the most complete and satisfying way, which is beating Alabama in the College Football Playoff final. To be the man, you gotta beat the man, as either Plato or pro wrestler Ric Flair once said.

Be it known, in fact, that by beating Clemson in their first game of the 2021 season and knocking off Bama in the last, these Bulldogs slayed five of the last six national champions. There will be no hint of fluke upon this title.

Having a team capable of beating the Nick Saban brand – college football's Apple, Amazon and Berkshire Hathaway combined – meant nothing until now. Hadn't Georgia almost done it in the last game of the 2017 season, watching the Tide repurpose a second-and-26 into a 41-yard touchdown pass in overtime? Just 11 months later, another last-gasp loss in a season-shaping SEC championship meeting. And, again, this season at a Mercedes-Benz Stadium-based conference championship, only this one wasn't close as the Tide took what was considered an ironclad Georgia defense and treated it like tissue. The Bulldogs were 0 for their last 7 encounters with the empire.

This time, however, losing once in a season to Bama wasn't fatal. Having stockpiled a year's worth of ratings goodwill by cutting through lesser SEC competition like a deli blade through bologna, Georgia earned a second swing against the Crimson menace in Indy. Everyone with eyes knew the Bulldogs to be the only other

Georgia cheerleading team members celebrate after the Bulldogs won the 2022 College Football Playoff National Championship at Lucas Oil Stadium in Indianapolis. (Hyosub Shin/The Atlanta Journal-Constitution)

opponent in Alabama's weight class this season and a rematch in the CFP final was all but preordained.

Why was it this team that finally broke free of the tyranny of Saban?

They will tell you about the special bond between the players on this team, that they were made stronger for their commitment to each other. And who doesn't love a good brotherhood tale?

As Smart laid out in that first press conference, he did go forth and recruit with a missionary's fervor. One great recruiting class stacked upon another, the wood that one day would fuel a great bonfire. The ultimate payoff was the same kind of depth of talent that Smart had enjoyed during his days as the implementer of defense for Saban at Alabama. And that wealth of elite ability made itself particularly known on Georgia's defense, which so often

played more fiercely than any in memory.

At the same time, though, wasn't it a one-time throw-away quarterback, one who had to keep coming back to Georgia like a stray you just couldn't shoo away, who led a national championship offense? Stetson Bennett IV proved that not everything about winning is plotted on the recruiter's whiteboard, that providence demands its role, too.

Another flashback here to that December when Smart was introduced as the Bulldogs' new guy. This time it was then-Athletic Director Greg McGarity, who looked out at his audience and said, "We have to believe we can do remarkable things here. There's no question with the potential here that great things can happen."

That had the ring of wishfulness then.

It holds the clear peal of truth today. ∎

CFP NATIONAL CHAMPIONSHIP

GEORGIA 33, ALABAMA 18

January 10, 2022 • Indianapolis, Indiana

GLORY, GLORY

The Drought Is Over: Georgia Is National Champion Again

By Chip Towers

"Look at the confetti falling from the roof! Look at the confetti falling from the roof!"

Surely, the angels in heaven were hearing that from the great Larry Munson on Monday night as the Georgia Bulldogs finally won that oh-so-elusive national championship at Lucas Oil Stadium. Gone now since 2011, Munson was the last Georgia play-by-play broadcaster to call a national championship victory for the Bulldogs.

Forty-one years later, that earthly honor fell to Scott Howard, Munson's longtime sidekick and the man calling the Dogs every year since Munson dropped the mic. His punctuating words will now enter UGA's annals for perpetuity.

"Dogs are winners; a national championship for a new generation of Bulldogs," Howard exclaimed. "How 'bout that final score, 33-18."

It'd been since the 1980 team went undefeated and beat mighty Notre Dame 17-10 in the Sugar Bowl on Jan. 1, 1981 that Georgia hoisted a national championship trophy. Monday night, against Nick Saban's mighty No. 1-ranked Alabama team, Kirby Smart's sixth team earned that right with a victory over Alabama.

Smart, himself a Georgia football letterman and lifelong fan, also paid homage to Munson in his postgame remarks.

"There's going to be some property destroyed in Indianapolis tonight!" Smart said from winner's platform, a reference to Munson's final call from the 1980 win over Florida. "This is surreal!"

The feat – accomplished exactly 14,984 days after the last one – was as steely as any we've seen from the Bulldogs. They overcame a mountain of setbacks and missteps, then did everything right over the final 10 minutes of play, both offensively and defensively.

Who to credit the most is a fool's game. Quarterback Stetson Bennett, dogged by Alabama's defense all game and Georgia fans all season, led the Bulldogs on a pair of fourth-quarter touchdown drives to make this a come-from-behind victory. The former walk-on and redshirt senior from Blackshear went 17-for-26 for 224 yards and two TDs. He improves to 14-3 as Georgia's starting quarterback, including 11-1 this season.

His performance came after being sacked five times, two of them the result of being called for intentional-grounding penalties.

Quarterback Stetson Bennett attempts a pass while under pressure from the Alabama Crimson Tide during the first quarter. (Hyosub Shin/The Atlanta Journal-Constitution)

The second of those set up Alabama for a touchdown that put them ahead 18-13 with 10:14 to play.

"I just put my head down and said I was not going to be the reason we lost this game," said Bennett.

He wasn't. He was a big reason the Bulldogs won it.

The winning score actually came on the next possession when Bennett reared back and hit freshman Adonai Mitchell with a 40-yard scoring strike. Tightly covered by Alabama's Khyree Jackson, Mitchell simply won the ball away from his defender. That gave the Bulldogs a 19-18 lead with 8:09 to play. A two-point try failed.

But after Georgia's defense got the ball right back for Bennett, he led them down the field again. Helped by an interference call, he hit the fabulous freshman tight end Brock Bowers on the gutsiest play call of the night. On third-and-one, Bennett faked the handoff and tossed the ball to a wide-open Bowers in the left flat. The Bulldogs kicked the PAT this time to increase the lead to 26-18.

And finally, Kelee Ringo intercepted Bryce Young and returned it a championship-game record 79 yards for the

Opposite: Wide receiver George Pickens makes a long first-down catch for an early gain. Above: Defensive back Christopher Smith tackles Alabama wide receiver Jameson Williams for a one-yard loss in the first quarter. (Curtis Compton/The Atlanta Journal-Constitution)

final score. Smart actually ran part of the way down the field following the redshirt freshman cornerback. But not for the reason folks might think.

"The sad thing is I was actually screaming at him to get down," Smart said with a grin. "All I was thinking was for him to get down so we could run out the clock and win this game. But he did the right thing because it put us up two scores."

Safety Lewis Cine was named defensive MVP for the Bulldogs. He had seven tackles and a pass breakup and was calling the shots from the back end of a defense that will go down as one of the greatest of this century.

After failing to sack Young even once in the previous matchup, Georgia recorded four on this night. After failing to cause a turnover the last time, they created two this night.

"I definitely think this defense is going in the history books," Cine said.

The Bulldogs' win gave them 14 for the first time in school history. It also vanquished what for them has been "the Bama Beast."

Georgia came in having lost seven in a row to the Crimson Tide, including a month prior in Atlanta in the SEC Championship game and four years ago,

Above: Kirby Smart shouts instructions to his players from the sideline. Opposite: Cheered on by his teammates, Bulldogs running back James Cook breaks free for a 67-yard run during the third quarter. (Hyosub Shin/The Atlanta Journal-Constitution)

also in Atlanta, in the 2018 College Football Playoff championship game. Smart was 0-4 against Saban, who came in 25-1 against his nine former assistant coaches who became head coaches.

But for the 100 or so players that occupied a jersey on Georgia's roster, Monday's accomplishment was all about vanquishing the 41-24 loss they suffered on Dec. 4 in Mercedes-Benz Stadium. The Bulldogs went into that one thinking they were the country's best team, and so did Las Vegas oddsmakers, who installed them as 6.5-point favorites.

Remarkably, Georgia was favored again on Monday, this time by half as much. That handicapping was based, apparently, on the Bulldogs' resounding win over No. 2 Michigan in the Orange Bowl and the Crimson Tide being without a few of their key players.

It was the third time there was an all-SEC national championship game. Alabama won the previous meetings against Georgia and LSU. Saban is now 7-3 in title games.

"Just never beating them made it so special to me," Georgia senior running back James Cook said. "So many games we were so close and they just pulled it out. But we pulled it out this time. Just holding that trophy up was the greatest moment ever and nobody can take it away." ∎

Above: Brock Bowers scores on a 15-yard pass as Georgia took a 26-18 lead during the fourth quarter. Opposite: Bowers celebrates with Justin Shaffer after his pivotal touchdown. (Curtis Compton/The Atlanta Journal-Constitution)

Defensive back Kelee Ringo's fourth-quarter pick six sealed Georgia's victory. (Hyosub Shin/The Atlanta Journal-Constitution)

Running back Zamir White (3) muscled his way into the end zone to give Georgia a crucial third-quarter lead. (Curtis Compton/ The Atlanta Journal-Constitution)

The Stuff of Legend

Stetson Bennett Writes the Perfect Ending to His Improbable Journey

By Steve Hummer

You know that commonly uttered maxim that it's impossible to win a national championship with a walk-on quarterback? Well, if you have a cat, that is today's litter. And if not, simply compost the nonsense.

Remember all the breath wasted this college football season debating whether lil' ol' Stetson Bennett should quarterback the mighty Bulldogs while a five-star arm like JT Daniels rusted on the sideline like forgotten army surplus? All that was downgraded to piffle and tripe on Jan. 10 in the biggest barn in the Midwest, which is destined to be spoken of as nothing less than the promised land by Bulldogs fans forever.

Inside Lucas Oil Stadium, the one-time walk-on from the South Georgia mapspeck of Blackshear led Georgia to a national title paid for in decades of tears and fatalism, engineering a 33-18 victory over Alabama for the Bulldogs' first national championship since 1980.

Forty-one years ago, it was a running back from Wrightsville, its population also barely five figures, who was remembered as the everlasting engine to a title. Herschel Walker and Stetson Bennett today walk the same historical plane. Never have so many owed so much to places of so few.

Afterward, with confetti raining down upon the victors and the Georgia flock that had dominated the stands bellowing on, Bennett declared from the field, "These are the greatest fans in the world. This is the greatest team in the world. I love this place." Love of place has always been at the heart of his story, and now it is a love fully requited.

This night, Bennett was a single sword slaying two dragons: Georgia's almost pathological inability to get past Nick Saban's dynastic Crimson Tide (0-for-7 against it until Monday). And the nagging thought that maybe lifetimes would pass before Georgia would win another of those type of victories that get tattooed on stadium walls and passed through generations like a family heirloom.

Being the good soldier he is, Bennett would credit everyone else around him, especially a defense that continually denied Alabama the end zone long enough for the Georgia offense to get a few things right. He would look back at the fourth-quarter play that was ruled his fumble and not quibble with the call, but rather determine that, "I was not going to be the reason we lost that game."

From that moment, Bennett was the chief among multiple reasons the Bulldogs won that game. Trailing

Stetson Bennett soaks in the moment after helping Georgia football end its championship drought. (Curtis Compton/The Atlanta Journal-Constitution)

18-13 after Bama cashed in the recovered fumble on the Georgia 16-yard line for a touchdown, Georgia would not throw often over the game's final 10 minutes. But when Bennett did fling, he was perfect. He threw six passes, completed four passes, and the other two were big gains after the Tide was flagged for interference. Half of his completions were for touchdowns, the most meaningful one the 40-yard strike to Adonai Mitchell barely three minutes after the egregious fumble.

Bennett finished the night 17 of 26 for 224 yards, two touchdowns and no interceptions.

As he acknowledged other stories on his team worthy of script treatment, Georgia coach Kirby Smart was impelled to say of Bennett, "Five years ago he was delivering passes like Baker Mayfield against the scout team (prior to Georgia's Rose Bowl appearance against Oklahoma). There's a lot of guys that saw him on that scout team make plays with his feet, his arm whip and decision-making, and we were very impressed.

"But again, to think that it would come this far from that National Championship he was a part of there (a Georgia loss to Alabama, of course) to this one, man, what a story."

To call Bennett a walk-on at this point is a bit like trying to portray Secretariat as a former plow horse. But the truth is he originally came to the Bulldogs as a walk-on determined to play at the university that was his first love. He crapped out on that occasion, went off to subdued junior college success before coming back to Athens with a scholarship in hand just in time to be a scout quarterback. Now Baker Mayfield may envy him.

Bennett began the 2021 season as a backup to the highly hyped Daniels. But when Daniels was hurt in the second game, Bennett took over and wouldn't give back the job. Hence the popular fan debate between the two

quarterbacks that was the background static for the last three months. It grew all the louder after Bennett's two interceptions against Alabama abetted the Tide's SEC Championship victory in December.

But talk about a complete rewrite of that scene: Last month it was Bennett throwing a costly pick-six interception in a big game. Monday he was sobbing with happiness on the sidelines as Georgia's Kelee Ringo returned an interception for a touchdown against Alabama with less than a minute to go, locking down a championship.

"The tears afterwards, that just hit me. I hadn't cried in, I don't know, years, but that just came over me," Bennett said. "When you put as much time as we do into this thing, blood, sweat, tears, it means something."

He talked about wanting nothing more in the aftermath of this epochal night than to go hug his family. Others may have doubted, but they never did. "They're the ones who have been in my corner the entire time, always supported me."

While Smart reminded his players about the place in lore they had just assumed. "I told the guys in the locker room, just take a picture of this, because I think back to the '80 championship picture and seeing all those players and all these people that have reached out and said things," he said. "Our guys have accomplished that, something special, and as they say, they've become legendary."

The format's changed a bit since 1980. Rather than one bowl game leading to a title, now there is a two-tier playoff. In both the semifinal and final, it was a former walk-on who was named the most valuable offensive player. That is the stuff of legend. ∎

Stetson Bennett eludes Crimson Tide linebackers Will Anderson Jr. and Christian Harris during the third quarter. (Curtis Compton/The Atlanta Journal-Constitution)

HEAD COACH

KIRBY SMART

He's Smart. He's Successful. He's Also Underrated.

By Mark Bradley • January 3, 2022

It's the morning of Jan. 11, 2022. Georgia has just won its first national championship since Jan. 1, 1981. The Bulldogs beat Alabama 31-27 the night before. A gracious-in-defeat Alabama fan says to a UGA backer: "Great game, huh?"

Says the UGA fan, shrugging: "We'd have won by 20 if we'd played the right quarterback."

Says another UGA fan, having overheard the discussion: "We'd have won four in a row if we'd played Justin Fields."

This is, we emphasize, an imagined conversation. (The part about a gracious Bama fan was meant as a tipoff.) That's not to say such a dialogue is entirely fanciful. The run-up to the Orange Bowl saw Georgia's coaches having to defend their choice of quarterback. That quarterback would become the game's offensive MVP. Postgame coverage held that the unloved Stetson Bennett had Proved His Coaches Right.

But this, we also emphasize, isn't yet another in a string of Stetson-Bennett-Isn't-Really-So-Bad missives. We'll save that for when he's named offensive MVP of the College Football Playoff final. This is about Kirby Smart, the best coach ever to be deemed an utter imbecile.

This will mark Georgia's second appearance in the national championship game in four seasons. Smart was hired to take the Bulldogs where Mark Richt could not. (Had there been a playoff in place a decade earlier, things might have been different.) Smart's record as a head coach – which he'd never been before 2016 – is 65-15. His record over the past five seasons is 57-10. That's a winning percentage of .851.

And yet: His record against Alabama is 0-4. That's a losing percentage of 1.000.

Smart isn't the easiest guy to defend. If he has admitted being wrong about anything, the moment has eluded this observer. He's stubborn. He enjoys having the last word. (Name a coach who doesn't.) The fake field goal in Baton Rouge was a great call. The fake punt against Bama was greater still. It wasn't his fault neither ploy worked.

Still, Nick Saban lost to Auburn on a no-chance field goal that was returned for the winning touchdown. Saban saw a fake kick snuffed by Clemson in the championship game two years ago. No coach wins 'em all. John Wooden was in his 14th UCLA season before his Bruins reached the Final Four,

The quarterback debate was an ongoing storyline during Georgia's season, but head coach Kirby Smart ultimately made the necessary moves to lead the Bulldogs to a championship. (Hyosub Shin/The Atlanta Journal-Constitution)

which wasn't yet known as such. He would retire with 10 national championships.

We grade coaches on their records, duh, but over time their records are a function of process. Smart has done everything Georgia could have asked – dominate the SEC East, recruit at the highest level, hire capable assistant coaches – except beat Alabama/Saban. We note for the record that Saban is the greatest coach in the history of college football. He's also 70. He can't coach forever.

Smart is 46. He can go a good while longer. It's unknown what program will be the next Alabama – there mightn't be a next Alabama – but any list of possibilities must include Georgia. That's how well Smart has built.

Had Saban not changed quarterbacks at halftime on the night of Jan. 8, 2018, we'd view Smart differently. He'd have been a national champ in Year 2. He'd have answered the questions – about beating Bama/Saban – we still pose today. But that narrow loss, followed by another narrow loss to the same opponent 11 months later, threw open the door to second-guessing. Should Fields have been promoted above Jake Fromm? Didn't Dabo Swinney have the foresight to pick Trevor Lawrence over Kelly Bryant? Isn't JT Daniels a bigger talent than Bennett, the former walk-on?

All of which leads to this: Is Smart a coach who gets the little things right but botches the big thing? The belief here is that a coach whose team is in contention for a championship most every year will, sooner or later, become a championship coach. How long did it take Tom Osborne? Were Smart regarded in the industry as someone lacking in brainpower, would so many sharp assistants and gifted recruits keep hitching their wagons to his? Would those players perform with such focused fury and attention to detail?

Georgia has won 13 games in the 2021-2022 season. Only the first, against Clemson on a neutral field, was close. In the Bulldogs' loss, they led 10-0. Then Alabama – of course it was Alabama – came storming back, and we all,

Kirby Smart has in short order positioned Georgia as a powerhouse program in the college football landscape. (Curtis Compton/The Atlanta Journal-Constitution)

this correspondent included, wondered why Daniels wasn't deployed. Offensive coordinator Todd Monken said that sticking with Bennett was his choice, but nothing about Georgia football isn't subject to the head coach's veto.

Five weeks later, there we were again. The sport's dominant program against its closest facsimile. Teacher against pupil. Georgia fans – well, some Georgia fans – live in fear of the moment when Saban will do something smart and Smart will do something dumb. Still, it's noteworthy that the cold-eyed folks who set the Vegas line reinstalled the Bulldogs as favorites.

Smart makes $7 million a year. His administration has given him whatever he wants. His record tells us he's among the best in his cutthroat business. There's no way such a coach should be underrated by a subset of constituents, but doggone if that's not how it feels. ∎

Above: Kirby Smart celebrates after a dominant win over rival Florida, one of many comfortable wins for Georgia on the season. (Stephen B. Morton/The Atlanta Journal-Constitution) Opposite: Even with a great deal of success early in his Georgia tenure, Kirby Smart faced mounting pressure, but ultimately patience paid off as he captured a championship in his sixth season at the helm. (Hyosub Shin/The Atlanta Journal-Constitution)

GEORGIA 10, CLEMSON 3

September 4, 2021 • Charlotte, North Carolina

WINNING THE HARD WAY

Georgia's Defense is Great, but Kirby Smart Knows: 'We've Got to Score Points'

By Michael Cunningham

This was the moment for Georgia coach Kirby Smart to declare that, in this era of video-game offense, it's still possible to win big by getting stops. Smart has fielded great defenses for a long time, and this might have been that group's finest night. The Bulldogs had just held Clemson to the fewest points in Dabo Swinney's 14 seasons as coach.

And Smart did puff his chest a bit about his defense after Georgia's 10-3 victory. He noted that the Bulldogs aimed to hold opponents to less than 13 points every game.

"Everybody thinks we're crazy," Smart said. "They think, 'You're never going to hold anyone to under 13 points in this day and age.' Why can't we?"

Yet Smart also said: "We've got a really good, physical football team. But we've got to score points. Because defense is hard to play now.

"You've got to score points to win games, and we know that. We've worked really hard on that, and we've got to get better at that."

That's true. The Bulldogs took advantage of a young quarterback, DJ Uiagalelei. Yet it's also the case that Georgia's defense is always elite under Smart. As he said, why can't they suffocate opponents like this?

The Tigers really couldn't do anything at all. They didn't break 100 total yards until their 10th possession. By that point they had five three-and-outs, including three drives for negative yards.

The Bulldogs rattled Uiagalelei. He's the successor to Trevor Lawrence, the No. 1 pick in the last NFL draft. Uiagalelei was a big-time recruit and played well while replacing Lawrence for two starts as a freshman. He didn't play a defense as good as Georgia's.

The Bulldogs sacked Uiagalelei seven times and never let him get comfortable in the pocket. When he did have time to throw, Georgia's pass coverage made him hesitant to let it fly. Clemson never could take pressure off of him by running the ball.

"I think we frustrated them and confused them," Smart said.

The Bulldogs cashed in on Uiagalelei's first big mistake, in the second quarter. Cornerback Christopher Smith baited Uiagalelei into throwing inside to Ross on third down and beat Ross to the spot. Smith snagged the ball and was in the clear to run 74 yards for a touchdown.

Georgia's offense was having a hard time, too. Clemson's defense slipped last season, which means

Georgia linebacker Channing Tindall (41) was part of a suffocating effort in the win against Clemson, holding them to a mere field goal on 180 total yards. (Curtis Compton/The Atlanta Journal-Constitution)

it was just very good instead of dominant. The group looked to be back to its usual standards in the opener. It just didn't matter much because Clemson couldn't score.

"If the defense does that every game, we don't need to score more than four points," Bulldogs quarterback JT Daniels said.

Through three quarters Clemson never got closer than 33 yards from Georgia's end zone. And that was courtesy of its defense. Baylon Spector intercepted Daniels' pass to end Georgia's first drive after halftime. Then the Tigers lost nine yards on three plays, two of them sacks, before punting.

The Bulldogs produced three punts and a field goal in the first half. Like Uiagalelei, Daniels frequently had pass rushers in his face. He showed good awareness to get the ball out quick. The interception was his only bad decision.

The Bulldogs didn't throw deep much.

"They played some soft zone," Smart said. "They didn't give us a lot of shots."

Georgia's offense didn't really need to take many chances. Its defense was giving Clemson nothing. The Bulldogs extended their lead to 10-3 in the fourth quarter by going 81 yards on 11 plays. That seemed to be plenty enough points, but suddenly the Tigers found a rhythm in the fourth quarter.

Uiagalelei and wide receiver Joseph Ngata connected for a 44-yard gain on third-and-nine. That put the Tigers at Georgia's 42-yard line. A defensive pass-interference penalty set up a first-and-goal. Georgia twice pressured Uiagalelei until he threw it away, and Latavious Brini broke up another pass.

Clemson kicked a field goal to reduce its deficit to a touchdown. The clock showed 9:08 left. The Bulldogs would have to finish. They couldn't gain a first down on their next drive. Clemson nearly bailed them out with a penalty for running into the punter.

The Tigers gained two first downs to make it to midfield. Jordan Davis, Georgia's massive-but-quick nose tackle, sacked Uiagalelei on first down. Safety Lewis

Cine broke up Uiagalelei's pass on third down. The Bulldogs sent multiple blitzers at Uiagalelei on fourth-and-5. He rushed the throw and it fell incomplete.

The Bulldogs closed out the victory by running the ball. They won a physical game in which both offenses wheezed. The teams played to a stalemate at the line of scrimmage.

The punters were making the best plays. Then came Smith's lightning bolt out of nowhere. It turned out that was all the points Georgia needed to beat the Tigers.

The Bulldogs were, of course, happy for that. They also know it's also the case that it won't be enough.

The expectation was that Clemson's offense would keep rolling with Uiagalelei and the other talented players recruited by Swinney. That belief grew when star wide receiver Justyn Ross was cleared to play after missing the previous season with a neck injury. But that's a lot to put on Uiagalelei because, really, how often do inexperienced quarterbacks step in and immediately play well for elite teams?

Lawrence did it for Clemson. It's happening regularly nowadays at Alabama. It's not the norm at most places, though. Uiagalelei might eventually be great, but he wasn't ready for Georgia.

Speaking of the Crimson Tide, people had them on their minds. As fans streamed into Bank of America Stadium, No. 1 Alabama was finishing its blowout victory over No. 14 Miami at Mercedes-Benz Stadium. The Tide saw nearly half of their offensive starters from last season selected in the first two rounds of the NFL draft. They opened their national title defense by hanging 44 points on the Hurricanes like it was nothing.

Georgia will have to deal with the Alabama machine to get where they want to go. The Bulldogs have the defense to do it. Figure how to score more points, and they'll be a challenge for Bama should they see each other again in the postseason. ∎

Nakobe Dean made his presence felt in a big way in the win over Clemson, with five tackles and two sacks. (Curtis Compton/The Atlanta Journal-Constitution)

29

DEFENSIVE BACK

CHRISTOPHER SMITH

Smith Recognized by SEC for Pivotal Play in Victory Over Clemson

By Chip Towers • September 7, 2021

When Christopher Smith was named SEC Defensive Player of the Week, the least surprised person in Georgia was Winston Gordon.

Gordon was Smith's high school coach at Hapeville Charter Academy, and he's been preaching that it's just a matter of time for Smith since he showed up at his school in 2016.

"Chris Smith is a phenomenal person, man; let's get past the athlete part of it," Gordon said.

"Chris Smith was a leader in the classroom here, graduated in the top 25 percent of his class, made well over a 1,000 on his SAT."

Smith turned in the biggest play of the game in Georgia's 10-3 win over then-No. 3 Clemson. Late in the second quarter, he stepped in front of a DJ Uiagalelei pass for Justyn Ross and returned it 74 yards for the first and only touchdown in what will go down as one of the top matchups in college football this season.

Smith also had three tackles in the game and played a major role in a Georgia defensive effort that limited the Tigers to 186 yards of total offense, two yards rushing and seven sacks. Clemson had gained 400 or more yards in its previous 12 games.

What made the defensive effort in that game particularly pleasing for the Bulldogs was they did it with three senior defensive backs who had not played prominent on-field roles on the team until this season.

Smith is somewhat of an exception in that regard. He was pressed into service last season after Richard LeCounte almost was killed in a midseason motorcycle accident and was lost for the season. Smith started the last five games of the season and played extremely well, with 26 tackles and four quarterback pressures.

He picked up his first career interception and touchdown against Clemson. That probably doesn't happen if Smith is not a wily senior who knew exactly what was going to be coming on a third-and-4 play at the Georgia 30 in a scoreless game with barely three minutes to go in the first half.

Smith knew Uiagalelei would be looking for Ross on an underneath route in that scenario. Smith baited Ross by feigning outside leverage before the snap, then crashed hard inside the hashmarks to beat Ross to the spot when the football was released. Smith never broke stride after snatching away the pass, and he outran the angled pursuit of Uiagelelei down the Clemson sideline.

"That was the whole point of the play," Smith said

Christopher Smith made a huge play in the second quarter of the win over Clemson, intercepting a pass and returning it for a touchdown in what proved to be the decisive score of the game. (Curtis Compton/The Atlanta Journal-Constitution)

when asked if he was baiting the quarterback to make that throw. "We ran that play a thousand times during the fall and spring and summer. We'd been working on a disguise, and (Latavious) Brini did a great job of holding inside and showing blitz. I showed outside and jumped inside, and it was the perfect combination. He threw it right to me."

Georgia was able to execute such a play only because of the veteran experience it has in its secondary. The Bulldogs are paper thin in the back end of their defense. But with the exception of junior safety Lewis Cine, they're an all-senior group which includes Brini and Ameer Speed.

Georgia has lost defensive backs Tyrique Stevenson (Miami), Major Burns (LSU), Otis Reese (Ole Miss) and Divaad Wilson (Central Florida) to transfers the past couple of seasons.

Fortunately for the Bulldogs, guys like Smith, Speed and Brini opted to stay.

"I believe if you believe in yourself and believe in all the hard work you're putting in, good things will come to you," said Brini, a 6-foot-2, 210-pound native of Miami. "I'm a hard worker, and I just believe in myself."

Same for Smith. Gordon said the senior never brought up to him the possibility of transferring.

"Not one of my kids have had a situation where they went to the transfer portal," Gordon said proudly. "They have hung in there and fought their situations out. Not one time has Chris Smith mentioned that he wanted to leave. Not one time. He cut off his recruitment once he committed to Georgia, and he's stuck with it ever since."

"He's a great, great human being, first; I keep telling people that," Gordon added. "He never had an inkling to leave the University of Georgia and go anywhere else." ■

While several teammates in the secondary utilized the transfer portal and departed Georgia in recent years, Christopher Smith was patient in waiting for his opportunity and it paid off in a big way. (Curtis Compton/The Atlanta Journal-Constitution)

GEORGIA 56, UAB 7

September 11, 2021 • Athens, Georgia

THE MAN FOR THE MOMENT

Bennett Leads UGA to Runaway Win Over UAB

By Mark Bradley

If you guessed Stetson Bennett would start Game 2 for the No. 2 team in these United States … well, your name is probably Stetson Fleming Bennett IV, the little man who won't go away. He believes in himself, even if he's the only one. He keeps hanging around Athens – OK, he spent a season at a Mississippi JUCO – when any other self-respecting quarterback would have been done with Georgia long ago.

Here, though, is a stat SBF IV can wear with pride. Over his extended time in Athens – he arrived in 2017, when Jake Fromm did; he was one year behind Jacob Eason, one year ahead of Justin Fields – he has started six games. Georgia has won four. The exceptions came at Alabama last year after Georgia led at halftime and against Florida on a day Bennett hurt his shoulder.

He's not Eason or Fromm or Fields. He's not JT Daniels. Still, Bennett is a fine guy to have around. Crafty Kirby Smart allowed the watching world to believe Carson Beck would start if Daniels, who tweaked an oblique against Clemson in Charlotte, couldn't go. Instead Georgia deputized Bennett, again, and the team that didn't manage a touchdown in its opener came out and looked like LSU circa 2019.

Fifty-one seconds into the second quarter against UAB, a resuscitated program that prides itself on defense, Bennett had thrown for 245 yards and four touchdowns. Such performances won Joe Burrow a Heisman Trophy. Bennett will not win the Heisman. Heck, he mightn't start another game. No matter. He was flat-out tremendous on a day when the nation's No. 2 team played as if it had a point to prove. That team would win 56-7.

On the game's second snap – you might have missed it, ESPN opting to bump UGA-UAB to its online platform while waiting for South Carolina and Tennessee to finish their games – the surprise starter faked a handoff and threw long for Jermaine Burton. The team that hadn't scored an offensive touchdown over 60 minutes against Clemson needed 38 seconds and 73 yards to rectify that. Then Bennett threw another TD, this to Kenny McIntosh for 12 yards. Then Bennett really got going.

Freshman tight end Brock Bowers ran under a sideline throw and went the distance, which proved quite a distance – 89 yards. Then Bennett threw long again, this delivery finding the waiting arms of wideout Arian Smith, another frosh. (As we know, Bennett is known as the Mailman.) Toward half's end, he felt the need to redeem himself – he'd just thrown his first incompletion – and did so by finding Bowers again to make the score 35-nil.

Bennett's halftime stats: Nine passes, eight completions, five touchdowns, 269 yards. His final numbers: 12 passes, 10 completions, 288 yards. He averaged 24 yards per attempt, which is insane, which Bennett himself conceded.

"Seems to me that's an Oklahoma stat line when they play North/West Texas," he said.

Backup quarterback Stetson Bennett had a terrific day in relief of starter JT Daniels, throwing for 288 yards and five touchdowns in the rout of UAB. (Curtis Compton/The Atlanta Journal-Constitution)

Then: "I was nervous ... I didn't eat the pregame meal."

Which never once showed. Indeed, this was Smart's rationale at starting Bennett over Beck: "We thought it would have a calming effect."

His day was done by the third quarter, whereupon Beck re-entered – he'd played a couple of first-half series to no great effect – and threw a touchdown pass himself. He also threw a pick-6, which is the only way UAB was going to score.

You could almost hear Smart chuckling – not that Smart is given to unscripted chuckles – and saying, "That enough offensive touchdowns for you?" His defense remains world-class. If we wondered whether Georgia might overlook UAB, we had our answer in the first minute.

As for Stetson Bennett: It wasn't so long ago that 99.9 percent of Bulldog Nation was demanding that he

be benched in favor of Daniels. That finally happened six games into last season. Georgia hasn't lost since. Daniels is an outstanding college quarterback. But if we've learned anything over time, it's that a team is only as strong as its backup quarterback.

Georgia has a darn good backup quarterback. He mightn't be the people's choice, but he'll always be ready. He has made a rather astonishing career from being ready.

Asked about those Georgia fans who might have been less than ecstatic over his latest start, Bennett said: "It didn't matter to me what outside people were talking about. It didn't really matter to me what anybody else said."

For the record, here's what Georgia's head coach said afterward: "I'm really proud of the job he did. Nobody has done more for the University of Georgia than Stetson Bennett." ∎

GEORGIA 40, SOUTH CAROLINA 13
September 18, 2021 • Athens, Georgia

ACCORDING TO PLAN

Georgia Handles South Carolina, Keeps Pace with Alabama

By Michael Cunningham

There are two things to watch for in a game like this. You want to see how Georgia looked while winning against South Carolina. You also keep an eye on the other College Football Playoff contenders. After doing both, I still see No. 2 Georgia as the top challenger to Alabama.

There were sloppy moments for Georgia in its 40-13 victory over South Carolina. But the spirit was good even when the execution wasn't. The Bulldogs dominated South Carolina like they should. There was little indication they've gotten too big for their britches.

Before the season, the CFP odds pecking order was Alabama, Clemson, Ohio State, Georgia and Oklahoma. The Crimson Tide remained on top by surviving in The Swamp. Georgia is just behind. Florida made a case to be up there. There's a gap to the other contenders.

"It's a weird year," Georgia coach Kirby Smart said. "Not necessarily the Clemson (vs. Georgia Tech) score or Alabama – playing at Florida is a tough place to play – but ... upsets seem to be more prevalent. We're not immune to that.

"We are trying to heighten our awareness to the standard. 'Hey, are we going to play to our standard all the time or are we going to go out there and be flat?' It's hard."

The Bulldogs didn't relax against their overmatched visitors. History probably helped Georgia stay alert. In 2019, South Carolina took UGA down a peg by winning as three-touchdown underdogs at Sanford Stadium. This time Georgia had the game in hand midway through the third quarter and won by 27.

Georgia quarterback JT Daniels played well after sitting out the last game with an oblique injury. Daniels was 23-of-31 passing for 303 yards and three touchdowns with a pick. Georgia's defense leaked a few big plays. South Carolina otherwise did little while committing two turnovers and giving up a safety.

The Bulldogs are at Vanderbilt next, then Arkansas comes to Athens. The Razorbacks can't be trifled with. Georgia then has a big test at Auburn.

Alabama's first major challenge came against Florida. Last time that happened to the Tide: against Florida in the SEC championship game. They passed again.

Bama looked vulnerable both ways in the run game. But perspective is needed. The Tide won a conference road game against an 11th-ranked opponent.

The other CFP hopefuls either have lost already, scuffled against lesser competition or both.

Clemson was favored by four touchdowns against Tech. The Tigers had to claw out a 14-8 victory. Quarterback DJ Uiagalelei, the replacement for Trevor Lawrence, still seems unsure of himself. It seems Georgia's defense isn't the only reason the

Wide receiver Adonai Mitchell extends for one of his four catches for 77 yards and a touchdown in the easy win over South Carolina. (Curtis Compton/The Atlanta Journal-Constitution)

Tigers struggled to score while losing the opener.

Ohio State lost to Oregon at home. The Buckeyes had to score two late touchdowns to put away winless Tulsa. Oklahoma (3-0) scored its fewest points with Lincoln Riley as coach in a 23-16 home win over Nebraska. Quarterback Spencer Rattler, a Heisman Trophy contender, didn't throw downfield much.

The only possible knock on the Bulldogs is that they scored only 10 points against Clemson. That's hardly an indictment. Clemson plays great defense. Since then, Georgia's defense dominated Alabama-Birmingham and South Carolina while not allowing a touchdown until the Gamecocks were put away.

The Bulldogs started fast again. They scored touchdowns the first two times they had the ball. Daniels was sharp. Georgia's defense leaked a big play early, but limited USC to a field goal. The Bulldogs led 14-3. All was good.

Then Kirby Smart inexplicably sent in Stetson Bennett for Daniels. Two plays later, Bennett threw an interception that set up Carolina near Georgia's goal line. Bennett played great against UAB, and Georgia must keep him ready. But the timing of the QB change was odd: Daniels had just carved up USC's secondary.

"Stetson earned that right," Smart said. "It just didn't work out."

Georgia held USC to a field goal again. Daniels re-entered the game. Georgia punted to end its next possession before Daniels found his rhythm again.

South Carolina gained 18 yards before punting it back. Daniels moved Georgia into scoring range with three completions for first downs. The 11-play, 90-yard drive concluded with his 38-yard touchdown pass to Adonai Mitchell for a 21-6 lead.

The Bulldogs scored twice more in the half. They followed a safety with Jack Podlesny's field goal before the break. Georgia led 26-6. The margin might have been larger if not for USC converting four of nine third-down plays. In the second half, the Bulldogs lost a fumble and Daniels had an interception.

"Execution error on my part," Daniels said.

Smart: "We've got to get better. We're not where we need to be."

Those are the kind of nits that get picked when it is national championship-or-bust. Alabama is the measure. In the SEC East, Florida remains the main threat.

The Gators held Alabama to 331 yards, including 100 yards rushing (not including sacks). The Tide scored touchdowns on their first three drives, then went three-and-out on the next three. After halftime, the Gators rushed for 156 yards, scored three consecutive touchdowns and were 5-for-6 on third and fourth downs.

Good effort by Florida, but no one is playing defense like the Bulldogs. Their opponents ran 166 plays before scoring an offensive touchdown. South Carolina's Josh Vann broke the streak with a 36-yard TD catch from Luke Doty. File it under garbage time.

Georgia snuffed out South Carolina's chances soon after halftime. On the third play, Georgia's Derion Kendrick intercepted Doty's pass and returned it to USC's 20-yard line.

Tailback Zamir White needed just two tries to score from there. The Bulldogs turned a South Carolina fumble into another TD for a 40-6 lead.

South Carolina's offense did manage one big play when it mattered. USC trailed 7-0 when Vann ran free down the left sideline and took Zeb Noland's pass 61 yards before getting caught.

"They threw some one-on-one balls and beat us," Smart said.

South Carolina's next three plays went for no gain, minus-2 yards and no gain before the Gamecocks kicked a field goal. Georgia responded with its second touchdown drive of six plays and 75 yards. The first one lasted 2:39 and ended with James Cook's 23-yard run.

Georgia needed just 1:28 to score after USC's field goal. Daniels passed on all six plays and completed five. His 43-yard strike to Jermaine Burton put Georgia ahead 14-3. That's when Bennett entered the game.

The Gamecocks gained just 162 yards before falling behind 40-6. The Bulldogs had 408 yards at that point. The Bulldogs weren't always sharp against South Carolina, but they were dominant. They still have their eye on Bama. ∎

Running back James Cook had a big game against the Gamecocks, with 71 total yards and two touchdowns. (Curtis Compton/The Atlanta Journal-Constitution)

GEORGIA 62, VANDERBILT 0

September 25, 2021 • Nashville, Tennessee

62-0!

Ascendant Georgia Leaves Vanderbilt in its Dust

By Mark Bradley

Maybe you're like me. Maybe you've spent at least five seconds of your life considering the question: If Thor and the Hulk got into a fight, who'd win? (Answer: Thor.) And maybe, having pondered one cosmic issue, you turn to another. Namely, how would it look if the best football team in the land played the worst?

Answer: It would look the way the first quarter of Georgia-Vanderbilt looked.

After 11 minutes and 52 seconds, Georgia led 35-0. It had gained 208 yards to Vandy's 11. The Bulldogs scored five touchdowns before their opponent managed a first down.

This wasn't a day when the better team wore down the lesser squad. This was a day when all-around excellence overwhelmed across-the-board ineptitude. Coaches want their teams to play to their potential, no matter the opponent. Georgia came close to maximizing its resplendent resources in this first quarter. It did whatever it wanted. It gave the Commodores nothing. It entertained itself by allowing its receivers – tight end Brock Bowers, then wideout Ladd McConkey – to score rushing touchdowns.

The final score was 62-0. Had the Bulldogs felt the urge, they might have gone for 80 or 90. Starting quarterback JT Daniels was done before the first quarter ended. Backup Stetson Bennett yielded to Carson Beck midway through the third. Seven different Georgia players carried the ball. Nine caught passes. Vandy finished with 77 yards and four first downs. Take away three false-start penalties incurred by third-string Bulldogs inside the final eight minutes, it was close to a perfect game.

Said linebacker Nolan Smith: "We have a standard here. We try to meet that standard every game."

Then: "At the University of Georgia, we make practices harder than the game. It's (meaning the game) like an ease."

Said coach Kirby Smart of his team's preparation: "We played videos of Mike Tyson. We talked about playing to our standard and starting fast."

Asked if anything about that first quarter could be labeled substandard, Smart said: "Kickoffs." He was being serious. (In Jake Camarda's defense, he kicked off six times over the game's first 12 minutes. His leg might have been tired.)

Smith again: "We say, 'Nobody in our end zone.' That's our standard … I don't care if we're playing the New England Patriots. We let nobody in our end zone."

Vanderbilt didn't move inside the Georgia 20. Maybe the real standard should be: Nobody in our red zone.

Smart again: "The biggest emphasis for us is this trajectory we want to be on. Every week, we get to reset it."

He offered the example of an airplane drifting off-target. Georgia seeks to correct its flaws, infinitesimal

Running back Kenny McIntosh got in on the touchdown parade against Vandy, scoring one of the eight touchdowns by the Bulldogs. (AP Images)

though they might be, every week. Said Smart: "If we correct that one degree off, we can hit our target."

Since managing no offensive touchdowns in the opening victory over Clemson, Georgia has outscored opponents 158-20. Daniels sat out the UAB game with a tweaked oblique, which made little difference. Bennett threw five touchdown passes in the first half. The Bulldogs have gotten nothing yet from the gifted receivers/tight ends George Pickens, Arik Gilbert and Darnell Washington. Hasn't mattered. In September, no team – not even Alabama – has looked better than this.

This was a game that paranoid coaches – all coaches are paranoid – dread. You're on the road in the one SEC stadium that doesn't feel like an SEC stadium. Kickoff's at 11 a.m. local time. There's no way your team can lose, but you're still worried because … well, you're a coach. Smart closed his postgame media session by challenging Georgia fans to show up early for the Arkansas game, which has a noon kickoff in Athens. He said an elite team deserves elite, and apparently prompt, supporters.

The point is that Smart, who apprenticed under Nick Saban and isn't one to laud his team overmuch, has set a higher standard for his sixth Georgia team than for any of his first five, the second of which almost won the national title. He isn't backing away from the E-word – "elite." Heck, he's trotting it out himself. He mentioned it after Clemson and after Vanderbilt. He's not blowing smoke.

No team in this nation has a mightier defense. No team is deeper. No team – not even Alabama – has a better chance of winning it all. ∎

GEORGIA 37, ARKANSAS 0
October 2, 2021 • Athens, Georgia

CRUISE CONTROL

No JT Daniels, No Problem as Georgia Blanks Arkansas

By Michael Cunningham

Georgia coach Kirby Smart warned everyone that this wasn't the same Arkansas team the Bulldogs blew out on the road to begin last season. That's true. The Razorbacks finished 3-7 last season. This season they'd become the nation's eighth-ranked team with victories over Texas and Texas A&M.

But Smart's team is better, too, and the game was in Athens instead of Fayetteville. Arkansas couldn't handle the Bulldogs in rollicking Sanford Stadium. Arkansas was shaken from the start and never recovered as No. 2 Georgia rolled to a 37-0 victory.

Arkansas discovered that just being better isn't enough to beat the Bulldogs. The Hogs had to be great to have a chance to win. They had to hold up on the line of scrimmage to do anything at all. Arkansas got whipped up front and self-destructed with 13 penalties for 101 yards.

The Hogs weren't ready for a game like this even though their starting quarterback played while Georgia's didn't. JT Daniels sat out with a back injury that he's been dealing with for weeks. Smart said Daniels has a Grade 1 strain of the latissimus dorsi muscle. Daniels missed the Alabama-Birmingham game with an oblique injury.

"We don't know if the oblique compounded the 'lat,'" Smart said.

Smart said Daniels' injury is comparable with one suffered by Dak Prescott. The Dallas Cowboys quarterback hurt his back during a July 28 practice and didn't return until Aug. 25.

"We think we'll be able to get (Daniels) back, but we don't know when," Smart said.

Smart added: "I'm not losing sleep over it because it's beyond our control, and Stetson Bennett is a really good quarterback. I keep saying that, and people don't believe it, but he's a really good quarterback."

Smart said he was frustrated by questions about Daniels' status because he wanted the focus to be on Georgia's effort against Arkansas. The coach better get used to it. It's national championship-or-bust for the Bulldogs, and their starting quarterback is out indefinitely. That's a big story so long as Daniels is sidelined.

Credit Bennett for throwing five touchdowns against UAB and taking care of the ball against Arkansas. The Bulldogs can win big games with Bennett. Two of their victories in his starts came against No. 8 Arkansas and No. 7 Auburn last season.

Georgia offensive lineman Justin Shaffer celebrates a touchdown by running back Zamir White to make it 34-0 over Arkansas in what would go on to be yet another shutout win for Georgia. (Curtis Compton/The Atlanta Journal-Constitution)

The two losses were at No. 2 Alabama and against No. 8 Florida last season.

Bennett made his first start at Arkansas last season and passed for 211 yards on 29 attempts with two touchdowns. Bennett didn't have to throw much this time (11 attempts) because Georgia had its way running the ball (273 yards on 56 attempts with three TDs).

Said Bennett: "We knew they were just asking, challenging us: Can we run the ball? They said we couldn't. We said we could today."

Arkansas starting quarterback KJ Jefferson started the game despite a knee injury. Jefferson and his running backs spent much of the day dodging defenders in the backfield and struggling to function with the crowd noise. Smart's defenses always are great. This one might be his best yet.

The Hogs were in trouble from the start. Their first drive began with two false-start penalties and things didn't get much better from there.

Arkansas trailed 21-0 after a quarter. The Bulldogs scored touchdowns on each of their first two possessions and recovered a blocked punt for another score. Then Georgia's white-hot energy to begin the game dissipated. The Hogs never came close to rallying because they couldn't pass, stop the run or quit committing penalties (they drew three flags on one play in the third quarter).

There was a moment when it seemed Arkansas might recover. On Georgia's second drive, Arkansas stopped White for a 1-yard gain on third-and-2. White ran again on fourth down. Arkansas defenders pushed back Georgia's blockers and White got hit in the backfield.

But White brushed off the tackle attempt and ran three yards for a first down at the Arkansas 32-yard line. On the next play, Bennett lofted a pass to Kenny McIntosh for a 27-yard gain. Kendall Milton ran for a touchdown two plays later. The Razorbacks couldn't stop Georgia or do much of anything right.

After Arkansas self-circuited with the false starts on its first drive, its second possession began at its 7-yard line following a muffed fair-catch attempt. The Razorbacks couldn't gain a first down. They tried to punt from the end zone, but Georgia's Dan Jackson blocked it, and White recovered for the touchdown.

Georgia led 21-0 after running only 15 plays. The Razorbacks finally got something going with Jefferson powering for runs. He gained 14 yards to get Arkansas past midfield. Jefferson's 13-yard rumble got Arkansas in scoring range. But the Bulldogs stopped him for no gain on third-and-5.

The Razorbacks tried a 37-yard field goal and missed. The Bulldogs responded with a field goal for a 24-0 lead, then Arkansas went three-and-out again. The Bulldogs powered down for the rest of the half and part of the third quarter.

"We started lagging a little bit," Bennett said. "We didn't take (a win) for granted, but we weren't really as focused. We've got to get better at that."

Zamir White's second rushing touchdown pushed Georgia's advantage to 34-0 early in the fourth. Jefferson was done for the day. Georgia breezed to another big victory margin.

The Bulldogs haven't been tested since beating Clemson 10-3 in the opener. They are at Auburn next. Then Kentucky goes to Athens. Then there's the weekend off before the showdown with No. 10 Florida in Jacksonville.

The Bulldogs should be favored to win all those games if Daniels plays. They've shown they can beat tough foes with Bennett under center.

"We know how good we are," Bennett said.

Arkansas knows it, too. The Hogs are much better this season, but they weren't nearly good enough to handle Georgia's early surge at Sanford Stadium. ∎

Running back Kenny McIntosh contributed 57 yards to the 273-yard, three touchdown rushing attack by the Bulldogs. (Curtis Compton/The Atlanta Journal-Constitution)

GEORGIA 34, AUBURN 10
October 9, 2021 • Auburn, Alabama

ACING THE TEST

Bulldogs Tougher than the Environment at Auburn

By Steve Hummer

In a mostly lovely Alabama village, the Georgia Bulldogs had their championship mettle tested in new and meaningful ways. It would be a trial by desire and fire, their first true game this season in front of a full house set on full vendetta mode against them.

Teams and talents may shift, but if there's one constant that all of Auburn can bring to every home game against the Bulldogs for, oh, only the past century or so, it's hostility.

Well, the results are in. Georgia aced another football SAT against Auburn, this by a score of 34-10. This still had an open-book, multiple-choice feel to it. When do the questions get harder?

Turns out that 70 traveling Bulldogs vs. 80,000 howling Auburn partisans is a mismatch if the Georgia contingent happens to all be built like barn doors up front and has a depth chart that reads like a recruiter's Christmas wish list. The poor screeching masses never had a chance.

Are you elite yet? That's the weekly query to Bulldogs coach Kirby Smart. His answer: "What we were, we were elite toughness. And we were elite composure."

And in the process, Georgia also answered (again) another question that has settled around them like a fog that won't lift: If needed, can this team win without JT Daniels guiding it, be that the season's sixth game or the 15th?

One more time, with feeling: Yes, it can; Stetson Bennett being much more than an adequate caretaker quarterback who plays behind a defense that just takes the air out of a stadium. In this one, it was a matchup of Auburn's Bo Nix and Bennett, the excitable boy vs. the dependable mailman. One whose feet run at a couple of thousand RPMs higher than his brain. The other who has had to live with the backhanded slander of being a cool, composed "game-manager." Nix is more fun to watch. Bennett is more relaxing to watch. On this day, take reliability and give the points.

Oh, and the "game-manager" hit on pass plays of 45 and 60 yards (that one for a third-quarter touchdown) to Ladd McConkey. He also broke free on a 30-yard keeper on a third-and-2 at the end of the third quarter to give breath to a possession the Bulldogs just had to keep alive to make sure Auburn knew its place. Maybe it's time to redefine.

Bennett finished 14-of-21 passing for 231 yards and touchdown passes to a pair of freshmen, the redshirt

Stetson Bennett runs past Auburn defensive end Colby Wooden during another strong performance from the backup quarterback. (Hyosub Shin/The Atlanta Journal-Constitution)

McConkey and Adonai Mitchell, both who have rushed into the breach of injury. So, take your time healing, Mr. Daniels. Make sure every muscle fiber is happy. The Bulldogs can afford to wait on you, just as they are on an uncomfortably growing list of casualties.

"This was (Bennett's) first opportunity to come into this environment and play Georgia brand of football," Smart said. "He made a lot of plays, man. He hit the guys who were open and helped us in the second half by making a lot of run checks."

Offensively, it could not have played out more perfectly for Smart, as his team got back to hard-nosed basics at the end, the Bulldogs driving 64 yards for a final touchdown, 10 plays all on the ground. Of the 21 fourth-quarter plays the Bulldogs ran, 19 were rushes. They saved that convincing brand of dominance for the end (rushing for 165 of their 201 yards in the second half).

And about that defense ... winning the opening coin flip, Georgia deferred and chose to make its opening statement with that best-in-the-country unit. Hardly a difficult decision. Yet, there were the Tigers making an early pest of themselves with their first possession.

They ground out five first downs – two on fourth-down conversions – while stringing together a 17-play drive. Nix seemed to fumble near the end, but instead was assessed an intentional grounding foul. In this case, the penalty was a reprieve. Given new life, Auburn would kick a 24-yard field goal.

Here was another new experience for these lordly Bulldogs. A regular season was almost halfway done and for the first time they trailed in a game. By only three points, granted, but even that slight deficit seemed yawning in a season of large wins.

If you were expecting them to get all nervous and panicky, well, perhaps that code doesn't exist within this team's DNA.

Again, Smart provided the theme for the day. "Two of our DNA traits are composure and toughness, and I thought never has that been more evident than today. Composure. And toughness," he said.

With very steady hands, linebacker Nakobe Dean wrapped up an interception on a ball that doinked off the hands of intended receiver Sean Shivers. That set up a tying field goal. So, to recap: For the year thus far, Georgia has trailed for a total of 5 minutes, 24 seconds.

Second-quarter scoring drives of 70 and 78 yards gave the Bulldogs a cushion. But the most telling sequence of the first half came with 51 seconds left as Auburn lined up for a 24-yard field-goal attempt. Georgia's Derion Kendrick broke early from the starting blocks and was called for offside, way offside. Rather than hurting the Bulldogs, the penalty had the effect of baiting Auburn into a sucker play, going for the touchdown on fourth-and-goal from the 3. Latavious Brini flirted with the boundaries of pass interference, but nonetheless broke up Nix's pass to Ze'Vian Capers. Just like that, Kendrick's impatience became a blessing.

Having chased Nix all over the field, the Georgia defense should be given the week off from all conditioning drills. Rocky Balboa used to get his work in chasing a chicken. That was easier. The Bulldogs expended an awful lot of wind and sweat to come up with their four sacks.

Auburn did discover the end zone once, which amounts to a stinging insult to a defense that had allowed only one other all season. On the 50th reunion of these Tigers, they can grandly retell of the 78-yard drive they mounted against the 2021 Georgia defense, and make it sound epic.

The Tigers did all they could in playing Georgia tough enough to make the Bulldogs starters work a full shift. Their fans did their part in making the setting uncomfortable. But again, Georgia aced another test, and answered every question almost before it was asked. They now have outscored opponents 239-33 this season (133-10 these past three SEC games). It remains that the toughest game they've had vs. an SEC opponent this year came during this spring's G-Day game, a 28-23 victory for the Red over the Black.

Next. ∎

Georgia running back Zamir White (3) celebrates with teammates after scoring a touchdown during the second half of yet another comfortable win to start the season. (Hyosub Shin/The Atlanta Journal-Constitution)

GEORGIA 30, KENTUCKY 13
October 16, 2021 • Athens, Georgia

NO MORE KNOCKS

Stetson Bennett Lifts Bulldogs Past Kentucky in Thorough Win

By Michael Cunningham

There were two knocks against the 2021 Georgia Bulldogs during their rise to No. 1. One was legitimate: Georgia hadn't met its high standards running the ball. The other was a matter of circumstance: Stetson Bennett hadn't needed to pass the Bulldogs to victory in a tight game. Georgia's defense has been so good that none of that mattered much.

That changed October 16 at Sanford Stadium. The Kentucky Wildcats arrived in Athens billed as perhaps their best team since Bear Bryant coached them. They looked that way for a half. The Bulldogs gained a lead by mostly running the ball, but Bennett would have to make plays passing for them to keep it.

Those knocks against Georgia are no longer valid after this 30-13 victory. The Bulldogs ran for big chunks of yards against an unyielding defensive front. Bennett passed to put away 11th-ranked Kentucky after halftime. Georgia's defense gradually squeezed the spirit out of Kentucky, as is its custom.

"They play tough in all three phases," Georgia coach Kirby Smart said of the Wildcats. "They don't make mistakes. When you play a football team like that, you have to beat them methodically."

The Bulldogs did it. Next stop: Jacksonville to face Florida. The Gators stumbled at LSU for their third loss. It's a rivalry game so you never know blah, blah, blah. Let's be real: Georgia should beat Florida and every other team left in its path on the way to the SEC Championship game.

It's still not clear when Georgia quarterback JT Daniels (back) will be available. He's missed the past three games. Maybe he'll be ready after the off-week. The timetable matters less with each game that Georgia wins with Bennett.

Bennett was good against Auburn's tough defense. He was even better against Kentucky. The Wildcats came into the game ranked fourth among SEC teams, with 193.7 passing yards allowed per game. Bennett finished 14-of-20 passing for 250 yards and three touchdowns, with no interceptions.

Bennett's first touchdown pass (19 yards to James Cook) put Georgia ahead 7-0. His second touchdown pass (27 yards to Brock Bowers) pushed the lead to 21-7 less than three minutes after halftime. Bennett was 4-for-4 for 52 yards during Georgia's field-goal drive for a 24-7 lead. After Georgia blocked a field-goal attempt at the end of the third period, Bennett found Bowers again for a 20-yard touchdown that ended Kentucky's comeback hopes.

The Bulldogs had a 14-7 halftime lead that felt shaky even though they were getting the ball first after

Georgia tight end Darnell Washington leaps over Kentucky defender DeAndre Square for a first down during the 30-13 win over the Wildcats. (Curtis Compton/The Atlanta Journal-Constitution)

halftime. They pulled away by riding Bennett's arm. He was 7-of-8 passing for 130 yards and a touchdown in the third quarter, then 2-of-2 for 44 yards and a touchdown in the final period.

"We kept hitting them with the pass, and we kept calling pass," Bennett said. "It was a little bit more fun for me. We can be explosive when we want to, and we can run when we want to. It's just about execution."

The Bulldogs ran for 170 yards on 26 carries (sack yardage excluded). When they passed, Bennett was composed and accurate. If Kentucky's defenders got too aggressive, Bennett lofted soft passes behind them to tight ends and running backs. Bennett did it while playing with a smaller lead than usual.

ESPN's Bill Connelly noted that, over his first five games this season, Bennett attempted only 18 passes with Georgia leading by less than 14 points. Bennett had 10 such attempts by halftime against Kentucky. He needed only three passes after the break to stake the Bulldogs to a two-touchdown lead.

Georgia's defense took care of the rest. Unlike last season's meeting, the Wildcats tried to make plays passing. First-year offensive coordinator Liam Cohen mixed in some creative pass plays to complement physical runs. It was a good plan, but Georgia's defense is just too good: Kentucky gained just 156 yards on 48 plays (3.3 average) and punted to end five of nine possessions before garbage time.

Kentucky scored a touchdown with four seconds left. Even that drive required 22 plays. It was a hard day for Kentucky's offense. The Wildcats couldn't score on their first four possessions and had to convert three third downs during their first touchdown drive. They stayed in the game because their defense was making it hard for Georgia, too.

The Bulldogs punted to end their first two drives. They got an opening when Kentucky, pinned near its goal line, went three-and-out and shanked a punt to give Georgia a first down near midfield. UGA's drive started with Bennett passes to Adonai Mitchell (10 yards) and Ladd McConkey (15).

The next three plays: 2-yard run, penalty and a fumble by Bennett. Georgia recovered the ball for a 9-yard gain, but Bennett was grabbing his right arm after Josh Pascal hit it as he passed. Bennett didn't miss a play. On the next snap he zipped a short pass to Cook, who ran untouched for a 19-yard touchdown.

Kentucky netted two yards on its next possession before punting again. Having established that they could pass on their previous drive, the Bulldogs ran as they pleased on the next.

Second play of the drive: Kendall Milton for 35 yards down the left sideline. Next two plays: Bennett for 17 yards around right end and Cook slipping through a nice seam through the middle for 25 yards. Zamir White accelerated through an even bigger hole on the next play for a 24-yard score.

The Wildcats were down two touchdowns behind, facing the nation's best defense, with the home fans in a frenzy. Kentucky quieted them by converting two third downs. Then officials ruled Georgia nose tackle Jalen Carter forced a fumble by quarterback Will Levis that was recovered by Georgia. It was changed to an incomplete pass after a replay review.

The Wildcats took advantage of that good fortune. They went on to score a touchdown that reduced their deficit to 14-7 3:53 before halftime. The Bulldogs seemed on the verge of burying Kentucky when Carter forced the would-be fumble by Levis. Now they were in a tight game after they'd bullied every opponent except Clemson, the only one of their foes to have a halftime margin of less than three scores before Saturday.

Smart said he knew the Bulldogs would be OK when he saw his players' demeanor at halftime.

"The players were talking to each other, talking about composure, what can they do better," Smart said. "No one was really rattled."

The Bulldogs had no reason to worry. They knew that no opponent has done much against their defense. Bennett sizzled after halftime, and Georgia broke through with some explosive runs. There was nothing left to knock about the Bulldogs after this performance. ■

The Georgia defense smothered another opponent, this time holding Kentucky to only 13 points on 243 total yards. (Curtis Compton/The Atlanta Journal-Constitution)

'If They Never Score, We Will Never Lose'

Former Georgia Greats Line Up to Hail 2021 Bulldog Defense

By Steve Hummer • October 22, 2021

As an expert witness for ESPN, David Pollack studies college football almost forensically, breaking down hours of video and getting lost in the high grass of schemes and tendencies.

That doesn't mean that when he's watching Georgia play defense, the experience doesn't also connect with something a little more primal.

"I can't use the exact words I would usually use (when watching his alma mater on D)," he chuckled.

"It's mesmerizing. It's amazing," Pollack said, settling on more appropriate language.

The Bulldogs defense – its dominance spelled out by the paltry 6.6 points and 207 yards allowed per game, both tops in the country – has led a lot of people on a hunt for a higher adjective. And not just those around the fringes. Among the most impressed are some of this defense's most legendary predecessors, the very people who should be the hardest to impress. These 2021 Bulldogs hit so hard their ancestors feel it. And not by just those in the US of A.

There's Georgia's career leading tackler, the late-1970s vintage linebacker Ben Zambiasi, intercepted as he was leaving work as a golf greenskeeper in Windsor, Ontario. He doesn't equivocate even a little when he calls this Bulldogs D, "Probably one of the best defenses ever, if not the best, right?"

There's the defensive back who had five picks during that blessed title year of 1980, taking a break from his fall canning in the North Georgia hill country (his pickled okra always is a big hit). Watching these kids fly to the ball is like a tonic for old bones.

"They don't realize it now, but what they're going through and what they can accomplish is quite remarkable," Scott Woerner said. "They've inspired me each week as tough and hard as they play. I know what I experienced way back when, and to know they're going through the same thing gives me a good, warm feeling."

We may live in a time of offensive entitlement, when the old saw about defense winning championships flirted with obsolescence. Why, even the losers of the past seven national championship games averaged scoring more than 25 points per game. But here is a defense to once more balance the scales and restore a proud Georgia trademark that dates to titled times.

Why, it reminds Woerner of what Erk Russell, the most colorful and colloquial defensive coordinator ever, used to preach 40 years ago: "If we score, we may win. If they score, we may lose. If they never score, we will never lose."

"We had the mentality," Woerner said of Georgia's last championship defense, "that no matter how far they get down the field, they're not getting in that end zone."

Frank Ros, a linebacker, was the captain of the 1980 defense, the standard by which all Georgia defenses that follow are measured. From retirement in Kennesaw,

Georgia outside linebacker Nolan Smith (4) and defensive lineman Zion Logue (96) were part of a historically great Georgia defense. (Curtis Compton/The Atlanta Journal-Constitution)

he sees today "a strong leadership group of guys, and they really rally around each other."

"They have a common purpose, and they're really buying into it. That's what we had. We had a common purpose," Ros said. "We didn't want anybody to score on us. We'd bend, but wouldn't break. Inside the 20, we'd buckle down, and they do the same thing. They play with a lot of camaraderie together, you can tell. You watch them, they're excited and they're competing with each other, which is what you want."

It all starts up front with the 2021 unit, where the likes of 6-foot-6, 340-pound Jordan Davis and 6-3, 310-pound Jalen Carter bring to bear an overwhelming combination of size and quickness. "Without holding 'em, I don't think you can block 'em," Woerner said.

If light can barely escape from this front wall, what chance does a running back have? Ask Kentucky's Chris Rodriguez. The SEC's leading rusher gained just seven yards against the Bulldogs.

So good and so deep is the front line that Pollack looks at senior Devonte Wyatt, sometimes lost in the large shadow of the others, and declares, "He's the best defensive player in Alabama's front seven right now if you put him on there."

Then fill in behind the giants an even deeper collection of linebackers led by Nakobe Dean, whose calling card is a disciplined speed and an instinct to flock around a football. They all play an inordinate amount of time on the other side of the line of scrimmage and strip all the glamor from a quarterback's life. And they come at him from all angles – seven different players have at least shared the sack lead in seven different games.

For a guy known to regularly arrive quickly at the sternum of a ball carrier – like 467 tackles between 1974-77 – Zambiasi recognizes what sets this defense apart. It's so obvious. "Anybody who watches, it's their speed. And they arrive at the ball with a nasty attitude – it's really fun to watch," he said.

For a three-time first-team All-American and career sack leader at UGA – like 36 of them between 2001-04 – Pollack revels in the kind of mayhem he once so furiously

Georgia defensive backs Lewis Cine (16) and Derion Kendrick (11) swarm Clemson wide receiver Frank Ladson Jr., a common sight from a dominant defense. (Curtis Compton/The Atlanta Journal-Constitution)

Defensive lineman Travon Walker and the Georgia defense held eight opponents to single-digit scoring during the regular season, including shutting out three teams. (Curtis Compton/The Atlanta Journal-Constitution)

sowed. He's proud to claim kinship to such an easily relatable defense.

"They all play with physicality," he said. "All of those guys play with a level of aggression that's a lot higher than most. That's what you love to see. You love to see people putting hands on people and moving people against their will. That's my favorite thing about football – you get to move people against their will."

The return of defense to a starring role is bound to strike a harmonic chord deep inside any classic defender.

"I love it," Ros said. "The last couple years, you kind of get frustrated, but you understand it because it's such a wide-open game now. That's what makes it so much more special what these guys are doing – they're playing wide-open offenses and still dominating."

Looking ahead, past the rest of the regular season to the promise of possible championship games to come, the ESPN expert spotted certain challenges to Georgia's defensive dominance. Teams like Ohio State and Oklahoma and, yes, Alabama, could be troublesome if they're still around.

"All three have certain key ingredients: They can throw on time, they can throw in rhythm, they have great offensive philosophies and they have mobile quarterbacks," Pollack said. "We're not bulletproof by any stretch. Not beyond reproach."

Some are in a hurry to proclaim the 2021 Georgia defense as good, or better than, any ever to play there. "They are special – they're not just 'going' to be. To me, the only thing that's going to get in the way is themselves," Zambiasi said.

We'll leave it here with more temperate language.

"It's early in the season to talk about legacy – this would be the definition of rat poison for coach (Kirby) Smart," Pollack said. "If you look at the numbers and defensive efficiency and you look at the gold standard – 2011 Alabama – they're on pace to be something like that. A lot of football left and a lot of opportunities where things can change, but if they stay healthy on the defensive side of the football with those guys up front and the multiplicity of what they have with their scheme, it could be a magical run. Could be." ∎

Many of the defensive greats that have passed through Georgia have a deep admiration for the defensive unit, which is arguably the best in the school's history. (Hyosub Shin/The Atlanta Journal-Constitution)

GEORGIA 34, FLORIDA 7
October 30, 2021 • Jacksonville, Florida

CHOMPED DOWN TO SIZE

As QB Question Simmers, Georgia Rides Defense Past Gators

By Steve Hummer

So, Georgia beats Florida thoroughly, beats the chomp right out of them. In one afternoon it seems to avenge every old slight, from 2020's humbling loss all the way back to Steve Spurrier's first cackle.

Just imagine what the Bulldogs would have done had they played the right quarterback.

Not that it would have much mattered who took the snaps – if anyone at all. Not with a voracious defense that sucked the very marrow from Dan Mullen's Florida playbook. Three takeaways in the last three minutes of the first half – all translating into touchdowns – touched off a rout that ended up 34-7.

Still, if JT Daniels was as healthy as Kirby Smart let on, it would have been a hoot to see Georgia's best arm get some work against what figures to be the Bulldogs' last best competition before the championship tournament season. Why not at least make this a bullpen game, deploying multiple pitchers (sorry, still in Braves mode here)?

The Bulldogs world aches to see Daniels again. Of course, maybe Daniels isn't quite physically ready. That's the easiest explanation. Coaches fib about such things.

All else about the game went very much how it should have. The most common caution you'd hear from Georgia fans recently was some version of, "Well, you just don't know about this game; weird stuff just seems to happen in Jacksonville."

By every tangible measure, Georgia was superior in all ways to Florida. This was a mismatch in the making. All the Bulldogs had to be concerned about was some vague, misty sense of unease. Save that for your next audit.

We can report that nothing weird nor untoward happened – unless you count the exceptionally early exit from the west stands at TIAA Bank Field, the blue state where all the Gator fans lived. The red-staters in the east stands quickly followed when even throttling Florida became too tedious to watch.

Just as it has been and will be all season, it was the Georgia defense that set the agenda. A defense that leads the world in allowing fewer than seven points per game gave up one garbage-time touchdown and saw its average tick up only microscopically.

A defense that had been prodded by Smart to be more selfish – recording just one takeaway in each of its past three games – responded with a first half of

Running back James Cook celebrates after scoring Georgia's first touchdown against Florida. (Bob Andres/The Atlanta Journal-Constitution)

stripping and snatching that was startling.

Smart mentioned that during one of the "nugget" sessions where coaches challenge their guys with little, pointed bits of information, they went over all the statistical categories ruled by this defense. And then dropped the hammer that it was only 70th in the country in takeaways. "That offends our guys. I can't say that's why we got turnovers, I can only tell you that was our attempt to challenge their pride. It worked out this week," Smart said. It is getting harder and harder to find ways to prod this unit.

For much of that half, both teams were just kind of out there, doing their high-contact choreography to no clear purpose. When Stetson Bennett, Georgia's replacement quarterback (at least to these eyes, still), threw a drive-killing interception, downed at the Florida 2-yard line with 3:11 left, the whole something-weird scenario almost seemed plausible. The Bulldogs led just 3-0, and the Gators still believed something good could come of the day. Until the Georgia defense put an end to that nonsense.

Just two plays later, as Florida quarterback Anthony Richardson struggled for one yard more, linebacker Nolan Smith wrenched the ball from his arms and recovered the fumble at the Florida 11. "Some guys yelling keep him up, keep him up and I keep pulling on him," said Smith, describing the highly encouraged theft. Georgia runner James Cook slashed to the end zone seconds later.

Smith was here last year when the Gators put up 44 points and 571 yards on the Georgia D. Of this year's game, he said, "It was personal. It was real personal." So, he made it his personal property. For on the Gators' next possession, he gathered in a tipped pass that set up his offense at the Florida 36. Bennett's best throw of the day followed, a soft loft into one corner of the end zone, gathered in by Kearis Jackson.

To further drive home the point that this Georgia team will go just as far as an otherworldly defense can take it, linebacker Nakobe Dean diagnosed a Richardson pass into the flat as if he were the intended receiver. Jumping the route at full speed, he intercepted it and sprinted 50 yards for Georgia's third touchdown in a matter of three minutes.

Linebacker Nolan Smith intercepts a tipped ball intended for Florida wide receiver Xzavier Henderson. (Bob Andres/The Atlanta Journal-Constitution)

The Dogs led 24-0 at the half, and Florida was finished.

Looking at Georgia's bigger picture requires some attention be paid to the offense. For it will be needed in harder games come December and beyond.

"We didn't play as well as we had been playing; that starts with me," said Bennett, who finished 10-of-19 passing for 161 yards, two interceptions and a touchdown. Florida actually outgained Georgia by a yard (355-354), more quirk than consequence this day. "We got to get better on the drawing board. The good thing is, we still won 34-7. At the end of the day, that's all that matters."

Daniels was deemed the quarterback Georgia needed at the start of the season, and he remains the quarterback it will need at the end. Despite his recovery from a strained shoulder muscle – he hasn't played since Sept. 25 – Smart said he opted to stay with Bennett because Bennett represented "continuity."

"Stetson's done a good job," Smart said. "Probably the next biggest thing is that JT has not really been in practice as much as Stetson… We went with the guy who's been practicing the most, been out there the most."

His two picks notwithstanding, Bennett has been better than a caretaker quarterback. He has kept the Bulldogs moving forward in Daniels' absence, earning his teammates' full support in the process. "When you talk about trusting a guy, I trust him," Smith said. "Because he goes out there and works and puts his best foot forward. Even though it may not look pretty to y'all, he's getting the job done." All true. But wouldn't you still like to see some really pretty quarterback play?

For Georgia, there is no such thing as a bad victory over Florida. Just call this one a victory that squandered an opportunity to get the Bulldogs' best quarterback back into the flow with just a month left to prepare for bigger games that may well require his singular talent. ∎

Assertive play from Nolan Smith and the Georgia defense contributed to a 24-0 lead for the Bulldogs at halftime. (Stephen B. Morton/The Atlanta Journal-Constitution)

GEORGIA 43, MISSOURI 6

November 6, 2021 • Athens, Georgia

A BRUTAL BEAUTY

Bulldogs' March of Destruction Continues Apace

By Mark Bradley

The nation's No. 1 team spotted Missouri three points and won by 37. JT Daniels made an appearance, his first since September, after Stetson Bennett, the quarterback who some insist can't throw, threw for 255 yards in a half plus 2½ minutes. The Tigers called two timeouts in the final 23 seconds and couldn't score from the 1-yard line. Anything else you need to know about this one?

Georgia has gotten so good that its games have become bores. Not since Labor Day has anyone come within two scores of the Bulldogs. The Bulldogs clinched the SEC East with a month to spare. There's no chance they'll lose before they play Alabama (or maybe Auburn again) for the conference title and the No. 1 seed in the College Football Playoff. Should Georgia lose that game, it would still make the field of four. Oh, and its defense is a creature of brutal beauty.

There's nothing bad to say about Georgia, unless you're among those who believe Bennett can't throw, which he demonstrably can. (His is among the more remarkable careers in the annals of college football.) After dispatching Mizzou 43-6, even Kirby Smart couldn't find much gripe-worthy, though he made a modest effort.

Said Smart: "We started out kind of sloppy. We had a little lack of focus, especially on defense."

Then: "We didn't run the ball really well."

Then: "Some guys (meaning players) didn't feel it was our best effort. We were a little lackadaisical at times, especially on defense."

This was, we note, boilerplate stuff. No coach ever says, "I'm happy with everything everyone did today," because if that were so, who'd need coaches? Credit Georgia for sticking to business when it became clear a while ago that this team was talented and driven and attentive to detail in a way few ever are. Since Sept. 4 against Clemson, they haven't given any opponent any chance of winning. Maybe Alabama will be different, but Bama still must earn its passage to Mercedes-Benz Stadium. Georgia already has.

Said Bennett, who has, among other things, a way with words: "I guess if you look at our record, having that zero on there is pretty cool, but we're just trying to go 1-0 each week."

In his postgame remarks, Smart did mention that his team shouldn't "buy into the narrative that's out there," presumably meaning that Georgia is too good to lose to anybody except Alabama. This outside observer would say that these Bulldogs have stuck to its weekly tasks in a way few collegiate assemblages ever do, a way that would earn the approval of Nick Saban himself.

As his team has risen to 9-0, the thought has occurred that Smart is settling old business, sort of like – "sort of" because "The Godfather" was a film, with much gunplay involved – the fictional Michael Corleone in the montage at the end. Stracchi in the elevator. Moe Greene on the massage table. Cuneo in the revolving door. Tattaglia in repose. Barzini on the courthouse

Wide Receiver Jermaine Burton gets into the end zone past Missouri's Akayleb Evans for a third-quarter touchdown. (Curtis Compton/The Atlanta Journal-Constitution)

steps. Poor Tessio offscreen. Carlo Rizzi in the car in need of a new windshield. All gone.

Here's Georgia's list. Clemson, which had the temerity to win national titles with quarterbacks from Georgia: beaten 10-3. South Carolina, which hired former Smart assistant Shane Beamer: beaten 40-13. Arkansas, which upset Texas A&M under former Smart assistant Sam Pittman: beaten 37-0. Auburn, under new management: beaten 34-10. Kentucky, getting bolder by the year: beaten 30-13, the Wildcats scoring with four seconds left after calling timeout. Florida, which beat Georgia last season, briefly breaking the Bulldogs' hold on the SEC East: beaten 34-7.

The cold-eyed excellence of these Bulldogs has been so sweeping that, a year after his Gators made their seeming breakthrough, Dan Mullen could babble his way out of a job. Mullen has so wearied of hearing about Smart's recruiting that he attempted to shrug off the concept, prompting Florida – which pays Mullen

handsomely not just to snap at reporters but to sign the occasional big-time prospect – to cut off interviews before its titanic tilt with South Carolina, which likewise entered at 4-4.

We've been saying since 2017 that there's only one thing left for this coach and his program to win. This is Georgia's best team since that one came so close. It might be Georgia's best team since 1981. (Which was slightly better than its immediate predecessor, which won the national championship.) We've just seen that it is in fact possible for a team from these parts to win all there is to win. Come Jan. 10 in Indianapolis, the Braves could well have company in their title-taking.

Speaking of whom: Joc Pederson, wearer of pearls and prompter of bleeps, watched from the Sanford Stadium sideline. Oh, and there was another distinguished guest. Said Bennett: "We saw (Braves mascot) Blooper during the Dawg Walk. That got us fired up." ■

4

OUTSIDE LINEBACKER

NOLAN SMITH

Nolan Smith Aims to Become the Freddie Freeman of Georgia Football

By Connor Riley • November 16, 2021

Nolan Smith is a big baseball fan. Despite being a Savannah, Ga., native, his favorite team is the New York Yankees. New York's 2021 season came to an end in early October at the hands of the Boston Red Sox.

Yet the Bulldogs' junior linebacker found joy in watching the Atlanta Braves win their first championship in 26 years. In part, it's because his dad is a massive Braves fan. But he also enjoyed getting to see his teammates enjoy a championship run, one he himself hopes to participate in as a member of the Georgia team.

Smith further expounded on how much he appreciates Freddie Freeman, the leader of the Atlanta Braves, and all he did for his team.

"That's one of those guys that stuck out with that program. That's something we do here," Smith said. "A lot of guys stick around for fifth and sixth years. To see him win it and stuck the ball in his back pocket, I'll never forget that."

Smith isn't the most recognizable player on the Georgia defense. Jordan Davis and Nakobe Dean have earned national honors and All-America recognition.

But when you ask who's the leader, on defense – especially the vocal leader of the defense – there's no doubt that Smith is the man.

"Nolan is real vocal. Nolan is definitely an extrovert," junior safety Lewis Cine said. "When Nolan is in an area you are going to know because he is really loud. He cares about his people, he cares about the players, he cares about the coaches. He cares about everyone. That's the type of leader he is."

Smith's voice and enthusiasm constantly show why leading comes naturally to the outside linebacker. Wide receiver Kearis Jackson compared him to a microphone. Tight end John FitzPatrick went with "very loud" to describe his personality while Jordan Davis pointed to Smith's "bubbliness."

It's not just his voice that teammates bring up. It's the vibe he brings. To meetings, to practice and most obviously to the field on game day. And he's just as loud when he's congratulating a teammate after a big play.

"That's a big thing as a teammate," defensive back Ameer Speed. "Having that there, that energy, I feel like that is what brings us all together and closer. It makes us play better when we're connected and able to love and play for each other. It makes everything a lot better."

"You see it on film; he plays how he talks," Davis said. "He wants that life. Nolan will always be the guy who will bring it and you can rely on."

Smith has long been working toward being a leader at the University of Georgia. He was the first player

Georgia linebacker Nolan Smith is the vocal leader of the Georgia defense, fostering camaraderie and enthusiasm among his teammates. (Jeff Sentell/DawgNation)

to commit in Georgia's 2019 recruiting class, instantly emerging as the pied piper for a class that ultimately landed Dean, Travon Walker, Cine and others.

Before he got to Georgia, Smith spent his final two seasons of high school playing for IMG Academy. He was playing with some of the best high school players in the country, much like he is now for the Bulldogs.

Not only did it help sharpen his on-field skills, but his development as a leader went to the next level at IMG as well.

"He's always had leadership skills. He's very intelligent," Georgia coach Kirby Smart said. "Everywhere you meet people at the schools he's been at or the schools he grew up going to, they rave about what a great kid he is."

As Smith has grown as a leader this season, he's also gotten better as a player. Against Florida and Missouri, he's forced a fumble, recovered a fumble, came down with an interception and blocked a punt. His performance against Florida earned him SEC Defensive Player of the Week honors.

"I think the more he played, the more he's played, the more his personality has been able to come out," Smart said. "I appreciate his leadership and really his energy and enthusiasm he brings to work every day is what makes him a good leader."

Smith isn't Georgia's only defensive leader, only its most vocal. Cine pointed out that the Georgia defense wouldn't work if it had 10 Smiths. Everyone has a role to play within the group.

Smith's just happens to be the loudest. And his voice may help carry Georgia to its first title in 41 seasons.

"Nolan is the definition of a leader if you ask me," safety Dan Jackson said. "He's always amping people up. Some people say he's known for how loud he is, but I think that's important to have on this defense and special teams. When I think of Nolan, I think of a leader automatically." ∎

Nolan Smith brings down Georgia Tech quarterback Jordan Yates during the Bulldogs' 45-0 victory. (Hyosub Shin/The Atlanta Journal-Constitution)

GEORGIA 41, TENNESSEE 17

November 13, 2021 • Knoxville, Tennessee

THE RIGHT MAN FOR THE JOB

There Should Be No Doubt that Bennett is the Guy for Bulldogs After Blowout of Vols

By Michael Cunningham

Stetson Bennett knew where he was throwing the ball before the snap. Georgia's quarterback didn't want to tip off Tennessee, so he looked to his left soon after he got the ball. Then Bennett looked to the other side of the field for the matchup he wanted: running back James Cook vs. linebacker Solon Page.

Cook sprinted past Page and caught Bennett's perfect pass to the back corner of the end zone for a touchdown. That score just before halftime started the top-ranked Bulldogs on their way to a 41-17 rout of the Volunteers in Knoxville. It was the kind of play that should leave no doubt that Bennett is the quarterback the Bulldogs should ride for the rest of their national championship run.

If that play wasn't convincing, then look at the many times Bennett ran for yards when none were available through the air. That included a nifty 9-yard score that put Georgia ahead for good. See all the times Bennett made quick throws before the pass rush reached him or sidestepped it to make plays. Don't overlook the many moments in which he avoided danger by getting rid of the ball safely.

Bennett did a lot of right things against the Vols, and not many wrong ones. He's been doing that all season, really. Bennett began the day ranked second among FBS quarterbacks in yards per pass attempt and third in passing efficiency. He'd run for 216 yards on 27 attempts, a number that includes yards lost on sacks.

And yet there have been persistent questions about why coach Kirby Smart has stuck with Bennett even with JT Daniels healthy and available. If Bennett's great day on Rocky Top doesn't end that talk, then so be it. Bennett still will keep on quarterbacking the Bulldogs toward the prize that's eluded them for so long.

The Bulldogs finished 8-0 in the SEC for the first time. (The league went to eight conference games in 1992.) They are 10-0 for the first time since 1982. They've won seven consecutive games with Bennett as the starting quarterback.

"I'm not going to overthink it with Stetson," Smart said. "We are trying to go game-by-game to get him better."

Bennett was 17-of-29 passing for 213 yards against the Vols with the touchdown and no interceptions. Those are his season-high for attempts and completions. Bennett also ran for 58 yards on six carries, not including sacks. The rushing touchdown was his first of

Running back James Cook catches a touchdown pass during the first half against Tennessee. (Hyosub Shin/The Atlanta Journal-Constitution)

the season. The score seemed to settle the Bulldogs after their defense was on its heels for the first time all season.

Said Smart: "His feet were a big difference in this game, his athleticism. The play he made on the touchdown run was special. ... He can still play better. He can make (better) decisions and not try to make every play an elite play."

The Vols came out with a relentless pass rush that had Bennett backpedaling early. After that, he picked them apart with his arm, feet and smarts. Bennett again showed why Smart is right to keep him under center and Daniels on the sideline.

Full disclosure: I supported Smart's decision to stick with quarterback Jake Fromm over Justin Fields during the 2018 season. Georgia won big games with Fromm and Fields was a freshman. Picking Fromm was the safe choice but, in my view, the right one. It ended up looking too safe and very wrong.

Fields went on to star for two-time College Football Playoff entrant Ohio State while UGA made the CFP only once with Fromm. In my defense, I didn't have nearly as much information on the matter as Smart. His ultimate insider's knowledge didn't help him make the best decision.

That episode seems to color everything Smart has done this season with Bennett and Daniels. Can Bulldogs backers really trust him to handle his quarterbacks? That question echoed the many times Smart insisted that he believes Bennett is a very good quarterback and not just an injury replacement for Daniels.

Pedigrees also play a part in the perceptions of the two QBs. Bennett is a relatively small QB who, we are constantly reminded, is a former walk-on. Daniels is a five-star recruit from California who looks the part and once started for USC.

There also are the recollections of Bennett's subpar performance in some big games. He wasn't good in losses at Alabama and vs. Florida last season. Bennett wasn't sharp when Florida beat the Gators October 30. Also, Bennett hadn't thrown many passes when the Bulldogs were under pressure to put up points.

I get why those factors might make Georgia supporters nervous about what could happen with Bennett in the future. The Bulldogs will face championship-caliber opponents with explosive offenses and, in the past, they haven't been able to keep up.

But I don't see what Bennett has done in the present to show he doesn't deserve to start. I do see that he's a better quarterback now than last season and has gotten better throughout this one. He's a better runner than Daniels, which is no small thing in today's game.

I also think there's some selective memory when it comes to Daniels. He's had some shaky performances, too, including at South Carolina last season and vs. Clemson in this year's opener. The Bulldogs won those games by riding their running game and great defense.

How is that any different than what happened with Bennett under center against the Gators at the end of October? Against the Vols, Bennett made plays as the Bulldogs turned a tight game into a runaway.

"It was a more balanced effort, I thought, which is what you want from your offense," Bennett said.

The drive that ended with Bennett's touchdown pass to Cook began at Georgia's 10-yard line. The Bulldogs led 17-10 with 3:05 until halftime. Bennett expertly directed the up-tempo march while finding a connection with freshman wide receiver Adonai Mitchell. Bennett was 5-for-8 for 80 yards on the drive as the Vols unsuccessfully tried rattling him.

The Bulldogs got the ball first after halftime. A holding penalty set them back and they ran five plays before punting. Georgia got the ball back when its defense stopped Tennessee on fourth down 17 yards from the end zone. Bennett got the Bulldogs in scoring range with a 14-yard strike to Brock Bowers on third-and-10.

Jack Podlesny's 26-yard field goal pushed Georgia's lead to 27-10. Tennessee's next possession ended with another turnover on downs, this time at Georgia's 40-yard line. The Bulldogs needed one more score to put the Vols away.

Stetson Bennett (13) celebrates with teammates after scoring a touchdown. Bennett continued to prove his mettle as a starter in the decisive win. (Hyosub Shin/The Atlanta Journal-Constitution)

They got it with a touchdown drive that featured Bennett running for one first down and throwing for two, including a 21-yard completion to Jermaine Burton. Georgia's running game took care of the rest. Cook scored a 5-yard touchdown for a 34-10 lead. After Tennessee gave the ball back on a fumble by quarterback Hendon Hooker, the Bulldogs bullied the Vols on the ground during a six-play touchdown drive.

What started as a tough test for Georgia ended with another blowout.

"This is a tough place to play," Bennett said. "They've got an explosive offense and talented people on defense, and there are 102,000 people in the stands. We weathered the storm, and we just kept chopping, and you saw it at the end."

I saw that Bennett is the best quarterback for the Bulldogs during their national championship run. ∎

GEORGIA 56, CHARLESTON SOUTHERN 7
November 20, 2021 • Athens, Georgia

BACK TO THE MATTER AT HAND

Kirby Smart 'Knows What He's Doing' at QB as Dawgs Roll Again

By Mark Bradley

Georgia played Charleston Southern and surpassed 100 rushing yards in the game's first five minutes. The massive defensive tackle Jordan Davis scored a touchdown while playing offense. Georgia led 49-0 at the half. It won 56-7.

Enough about that. Let's talk about Kirby Smart.

For all his success, Smart hasn't been above criticism. Such is the way of our world. Nobody likes everything anybody else does. Often it seems nobody likes anything anybody else does. But I digress.

Smart's Bulldogs are the unanimous choice as the nation's No. 1 team, having received every first-place vote in the latest editions of the Associated Press and coaches' polls. Georgia is the only team in the land that can sustain one loss and still be assured of making the College Football Playoff.

And yet, and yet …

There are those who'll tell you that when it comes to quarterbacks, Smart doesn't know what he's doing. They'll point to Justin Fields, who has started seven games for the Chicago Bears as a rookie but who didn't start for Georgia. They'll note that it took losses to Alabama and Florida last year for the coach turn to JT Daniels, by which time it was too late to win the SEC East. They'll note that Stetson Bennett, the man who won't go away, is again starting ahead of Daniels.

And here's where I say: When it comes to anything involving football – and football is largely about

quarterbacks – Smart knows exactly what he's doing. Nothing about Georgia football happens by accident.

Sometimes you hear a coach say he wants his team to play complementary football. Sometimes you wonder what that means, given that a team's offense and defense are never on the field at the same time. A better way to define complementary football is to point to how Georgia has played in 2021 and say, "That right there? That's complementary football."

If Smart needed Georgia to score a slew of points to win, Bennett wouldn't be his No. 1 quarterback. Daniels, who has the better and bigger arm, would be the choice. But the Bulldogs have yet to allow an opponent to score more than 17 points, and they haven't been held under 30 since their opener against Clemson. They haven't needed 350 passing yards to win. They average 239 air yards, putting them mid-table among the 130 FBS teams.

It isn't that Georgia can't pass. The Bulldogs deployed four quarterbacks against Charleston Southern. Only Brock Vandagriff, the fourth-string freshman, didn't throw a touchdown pass. Only Vandagriff, who was 0-for-1, didn't complete half his attempts.

When watching LSU's offense of 2019 and Alabama's of last season, it was possible to wonder if running the ball and playing defense no longer mattered. Those ancient virtues tended to work best in tandem, but with everybody slinging it, nobody seemed concerned with controlling the clock and/or the line of scrimmage. Smart is very concerned with the clock/line of scrimmage.

Said Bennett, who took part in Senior Day introductions but who might well be back next season: "If you can't run the ball, it's tough to control the game. Being able to turn around and hand the ball off is something a lot of people don't value anymore, but it's tough to overstate it."

Georgia's defense stops the opponent and puts the Georgia offense on the field. Georgia's offense eats up yards and burns the clock, thereby giving the defense time to rest and advantageous field position. That's complementary football. Nobody spoke of LSU's defense when Joe Burrow was winning his Heisman Trophy or Alabama's defenders when DeVonta Smith was winning his, but it's noteworthy that the most-hyped Bulldog isn't a quarterback or a wideout. It's the 340-pound Davis.

Georgia's strength is its defense, which is so dominant that it banked a turnover on the play that resulted in Charleston Southern's points. Even if Georgia had Burrow or Mac Jones, it wouldn't look like LSU 2019 or Bama 2020. That isn't how Smart coaches. Maybe you think he should. Maybe he knows more about football than you do.

In the wake of the Clemson victory, we all figured Georgia would be favored in every remaining regular-season game. It has been to date, and the Bulldogs could be favored by 30 over Tech. Not once has a lesser opponent caught Smart's team unawares. Not once since Labor Day has Georgia been in position to lose.

With Daniels as the starter, Georgia was more inclined to throw. With Bennett as the starter, throwing is a lesser option. The benefit therein is that the Bulldogs are less inclined to fall into an early hole if they're the team setting the pace. And should they fall into an early hole – against Bama for the SEC championship, maybe again in the playoff – it can summon Daniels and let him sling it.

In the national championship game of January 2018 and the SEC title tilt 11 months later, Alabama beat Georgia because it had a reserve quarterback – Tua Tagovailoa relieved Jalen Hurts in the first game;

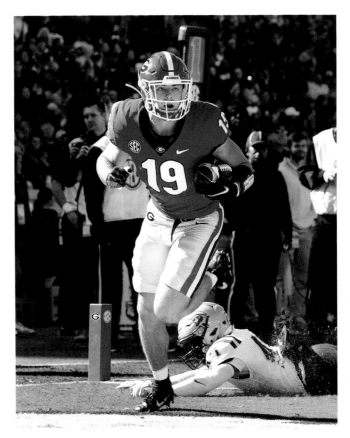

Tight end Brock Bowers makes a touchdown reception as Georgia raced to a 28-0 lead over Charleston Southern in the first quarter. (Curtis Compton/The Atlanta Journal-Constitution)

it was the other way around in the latter – capable of playing at a championship level. Pretty sure Smart was paying attention.

Smart has said Georgia will need Daniels to win a game before the season is done. Not necessarily to start a game, but to win it. Because of his arm, Daniels is more suited to being the comeback quarterback than Bennett. This, too, is complementary football. You've got one quarterback for when you're ahead, another when you're behind, assuming you ever are.

Bennett again: "A lot of people tell me that I'm living out a dream. The dream will be complete in January, whenever that game is." ∎

GEORGIA 45, GEORGIA TECH 0
November 27, 2021 • Atlanta, Georgia

THE CALM BEFORE THE STORM

No. 1 Georgia is 12-0 and Ready for Alabama

By Michael Cunningham

Beating Georgia Tech was a given for Georgia. Doing so convincingly was expected. The Bulldogs unofficially checked off both boxes by halftime at Bobby Dodd Stadium. If those aligned with them weren't already thinking it, they were by that point.

Beat Alabama.

"Everyone has had it kind of circled and seen it out there," Georgia coach Kirby Smart said after the 45-0 victory. "We've really tried to work hard on getting better. That's been the emphasis, is, 'What can you improve on?'"

The list is short for the Bulldogs. They are ready for Alabama. Lots of teams say that before getting more than they can handle. The Bulldogs won't be the latest. They'll take a complete team to face the Crimson Tide in the SEC Championship game at Mercedes-Benz Stadium on December 4.

Georgia has been the nation's unanimous No. 1 team for weeks. The defense is all-time good. The offense is on the come. Throw out Kentucky's last-second touchdown and none of Georgia's past 11 opponents lost by fewer than 24 points.

The Bulldogs finished 12-0 in the regular season for the first time. They say they aren't celebrating that feat.

"I hate to demean it," Smart said. "It's a big deal. It's an honor. It's great. But it's the next step in the process for this group.

"This group has had a single-minded focus. Never said, 'Hey, lets' go 12-0.' They said, 'Let's beat everyone we play, let's focus one game at a time and try to really dominate who we play.' And they've done that."

Now comes Bama, Georgia's toughest test yet. It probably would be easier to win championships without going through the Tide. It just would be more satisfying for Georgia to knock off Bama along the way. The Tide have ruined championship dreams for Smart's team twice in five years.

A victory in the third meeting would be a four-for-one for the Bulldogs. They'd win the SEC championship. They'd do it with a victory over Bama. They'd go into the College Football Playoff as the top seed. And they'd (likely) keep the Tide out of the CFP.

Before getting a chance to do all that, the Bulldogs had to flick aside the Yellow Jackets. They did so methodically and without drama.

"We were just focused on doing the duty in front of us," Georgia quarterback Stetson Bennett said. "We knew what this game means for the history of this program and that, if we slipped up, anything can happen."

Brock Bowers leaps above Georgia Tech defensive back Tobias Oliver for a second-half touchdown. Georgia's offense and defense were both in top form during the 45-0 win. (Hyosub Shin/The Atlanta Journal-Constitution)

The Bulldogs didn't slip up. The predictable outcome happened. Georgia scored at will, committed no turnovers and amazingly weren't flagged for a single penalty. The Jackets couldn't even manage a field-goal attempt. At one point I wondered if they'd gain a first down.

That's a preposterous notion, but Georgia's defense makes wild thoughts seem plausible. The Jackets finally gained a first down on their third drive. Then I contemplated whether they'd make it past midfield. That didn't happen until Tech's 21st play, by which time Georgia had scored 24 points on 22 snaps.

The Jackets ended up running 12 plays on that drive but gained just 39 yards before punting. It was a lot of effort for not much reward. That's been the outcome for every team that's faced UGA this season.

You can't chalk up what the Bulldogs did to Tech as them beating up on an outmanned opponent. Well, you can't attribute it only to that. Didn't Arkansas, Auburn, Kentucky and Tennessee look nearly as inept against the Bulldogs? Even solid-to-good teams appear overwhelmed against Georgia.

Said Smart: "It just says that they hold each other accountable, they are up for the task, they've answered the bell and they've done the right things. But we also haven't played a team the caliber of Alabama."

Bama was in the back of the mind when Tech made its first big play of the game. Jordan Yates threw over the top of Georgia's coverage to Dylan Leonard for 40 yards. Defending long pass plays is a weakness for the Bulldogs. In their case, that means they are just OK at it instead of great.

But Leonard's catch came with Tech down 31-0. The drive ended with Yates getting chased from the pocket on fourth down and futilely looking for an open receiver. The Bulldogs took over on downs. Two plays later, Kenny McIntosh was running 59 yards for another Georgia touchdown.

The Jackets never got close to the end zone. They really had just one playmaker for Georgia to worry about, Jahmyr Gibbs. The Bulldogs will have to account for many more threats against Alabama and their eventual CFP foe. The flip side of that is none of UGA's postseason opponents will have seen a defense this great.

Now Georgia's offense is peaking, too. The running game has rounded into typical UGA form. Bennett is playing better than ever. Freshman tight end Brock Bowers regularly delivers big plays. One of UGA's best wide receivers, George Pickens, made his season debut against Tech, just in time for the postseason.

The Bulldogs scored on each of their four drives. The first one ended with a field goal after a dropped pass on third down that would have gone for a first. On Georgia's second possession, Bennett was 3-of-4 passing for 61 yards and ran for first downs twice. That drive ended with his feathered 25-yard touchdown pass to Jermaine Burton.

Georgia's next drive: Bennett squeezed an 18-yard pass to Darnell Washington to Tech's 11-yard line, then found Ladd McConkey for a touchdown on the next play. Next UGA possession: Bowers took Bennett's crisp pass on the second play and ran the rest of the way for a 77-yard score. At halftime, Bennett was 10-of-15 passing for 226 yards with three touchdowns and six completions of 15 yards or more.

In the third quarter Bennett threw his fourth touchdown, and second to Bowers, for the 31-0 lead. He took a seat for the fourth quarter. The Bulldogs were on their way to their fourth consecutive victory over Tech.

"What we have done in this regular season is all good, but it's always about how we finish the season," Georgia linebacker Nakobe Dean said. "If we don't finish the right way, none of this really matters."

That's the spirit. Bring on Bama. ■

Georgia wide receiver Kearis Jackson picks up a long first down past Georgia Tech defensive back Juanyeh Thomas during the first half. (Curtis Compton/The Atlanta Journal-Constitution)

13
QUARTERBACK

STETSON BENNETT

QB Stetson Bennett Living Out His Dream with Georgia

By Chip Towers • November 29, 2021

A lot of people may not realize it, but Stetson Bennett didn't play in his first SEC Championship game when he started at quarterback for the No. 1-ranked Georgia Bulldogs against No. 3 Alabama.

Bennett actually played in the 2019 game against then-No. 1 LSU. He came in for one play in relief of starter Jake Fromm. Facing third-and-17 at Georgia's 34-yard line, Bennett threw an incompletion high over the head of Matt Landers. The Bulldogs, trailing 14-3 at the 6:54 mark of the second quarter, then punted.

Bennett remembers it well.

"When I saw Fromm go down, I just sprinted to my helmet, picked it up and I just felt this giant shock of lightning run through me," Bennett said. "'I'm about to go into the SEC Championship game.' I wasn't expecting that."

Fast forward two years and the redshirt senior started for the ninth straight game and 10th overall in 2021 when they faced the Crimson Tide in Mercedes-Benz Stadium.

"So, yeah, it was a little bit different," Bennett said.

Quarterback play will be one of the more interesting matchups in the latest Georgia-Alabama showdown, the fourth meeting in the last five years. Bennett has been around for most of that.

Including backup roles and a stint in junior college, the game was the 37th in Bennett's career. So, the former walk-on enters the competition wearing the label of grizzled veteran and blue-collar achiever.

His Alabama counterpart, Bryce Young, comes in playing the role of young phenom. He came to Tuscaloosa as a 5-star signee and was the No. 2-rated prospect in the nation in the recruiting class of 2020.

Many college football observers believe the 6-foot, 194-pound sophomore from Santa Ana, Calif., might have wrapped up his bid for the Heisman Trophy when he led the Crimson Tide on a 97-yard scoring drive in the final minutes of regulation at Auburn to send the game into overtime. Young hit John Metchie with the game-winning, two-point score in the fourth overtime, 24-22.

That was actually one of Young's more modest overall games as he finished with 317 yards passing, two touchdowns and an interception. But he arrives in Atlanta with some eye-popping numbers: 69% passing for 3,901 yards with 40 touchdowns and four interceptions. The Crimson Tide is averaging an SEC-best 42.7 points and 492.2 yards per game.

A former walk-on who also played a season in junior college, quarterback Stetson Bennett took an unconventional path to the national championship stage. (Curtis Compton/The Atlanta Journal-Constitution)

"They have really elite wideouts, but what puts them over the top is the distributor," Georgia coach Kirby Smart said of Young and Alabama's passing attack. "He is an incredible athlete, player, decision-maker. What he didn't get enough credit for is when the play breaks down, his skill set to deliver the ball, make people miss, set up rushers. He's like an elite point guard that can distribute the ball, and when he's dribbling down the court."

Bennett has played a little bit of that role for Georgia as well. His ability to run with the football while also drawing in secondaries with roll-outs and bootlegs has provided the Bulldogs with a dimension they didn't have when JT Daniels was at the controls.

Daniels, by the way, is quite familiar with Young. The two quarterbacks both played at Mater Dei High in Santa Ana, Calif. Young succeeded Daniels at that famous quarterback-producing school and, at one time, was expected to follow Daniels to USC.

"I've known JT for a while; we've known their family for a while," said Young. "That's someone that I'm close with and wish nothing but the best for. But, you know, in a week like this, especially for what the game is and for what everything means, I'm on Alabama, and he's on Georgia. So, for us, it's not a huge amount of communication going on."

Young's scenario is completely different than Bennett's. Georgia fans know it intimately: Kid from Blackshear raised by UGA-alum parents who took him to Georgia games every year since he was in diapers.

Bennett has shared before how as a little boy he'd dress up in his makeshift Georgia uniform and pretend to be quarterbacking the Bulldogs to a championship. He gets a chance to live out that dream against college football's perennial powerhouse program.

Now that he's in the moment, Bennett insists it won't be too big for him. He already played Alabama last year in Tuscaloosa. And while that wasn't a great performance for him – 45% passing, 2 TDs, 3 INTs – it remains one he can draw on and learn from.

Stetson Bennett shouts instructions during Georgia's regular-season win against Tennessee. (Hyosub Shin/The Atlanta Journal-Constitution)

"Stetson has been able to grow from looking back at that game," Smart said. "I don't know what that was, his ... fourth start. He's played a lot more football now. Certainly, he has improved in terms of decision-making."

CBS will surely revisit Bennett's story and might even show pictures of the little kid from Blackshear wearing the oversized Georgia helmet running around in the backyard. But Bennett says he won't be thinking about anything other than what he needs to do to help the Bulldogs beat Alabama.

"Yeah, I don't really worry about what other people say about any of that stuff," said Bennett, surrounded by microphones, cameras and a social-distanced crowd of reporters in Georgia's Butts-Mehre Complex. "My job is just to go out there and complete passes, get the offense in the best play possible and execute. So, I'll let all the story-telling and narrative write itself."

It has been a pretty good tome, so far. ∎

Stetson Bennett demonstrated growth throughout the 2021 season, from an early test against Auburn (opposite) to a 45-0 rout over Georgia Tech (above). (Hyosub Shin/The Atlanta Journal-Constitution)

99

DEFENSIVE LINEMAN

JORDAN DAVIS

Georgia's Jordan Davis Brings Big Personality to a Big Game

By Steve Hummer • November 30, 2021

No one has wrung more from Georgia's top-shelf season than Jordan Davis, the Bulldogs' Alp with feet. His holiness Nick Saban went on a rhapsodic riff about the man in the middle of Georgia's defensive line, anointing Davis, "one of the most dominant players in college football."

"If he thinks like that, I'm honored and I'm glad," Davis said. "But you can't let it get to your head."

The Bulldogs' largest player hasn't the ego to match. Another reason an interior lineman – the least glamorous and statistically rewarding position on the defense – has become the popular human trademark of the Georgia team.

Saban's compliment landed shortly after Davis had pronounced himself too big to be confined to just one side of the ball, running it in from a yard out for a touchdown against Charleston Southern. You just gotta have a yard, he's your man – there at the bottom of the Bulldogs' rushing stats you'll find the 340-pounder with two carries for two yards.

Whether Alabama need be concerned about this plus-sized rushing threat during the SEC Championship game, "I can't really say," Davis coyly put it.

"But if I get the rock, I'll try to make something shake." Most likely the foundation of Mercedes-Benz Stadium.

Davis would conclude his Senior Day vs. Charleston Southern by leading the marching band in a rendition of "Glory, Glory." If you spotted him grooming Uga or taking one of the majorettes' batons out for a quick twirl in advance of the SEC title game, don't be surprised. He seems intent upon visiting every facet of Bulldog life before departing.

Davis has approached this season with the joy and curiosity of someone who expected none of it. When he was spotted at a Braves game this season, recognized, and received like visiting royalty, it amazed Davis. To him, it's as if Georgia's rampage through the conference and his own spiking popularity is one big surprise party. So why not glory in every moment?

It's when asked why he is so committed to never getting cheated on any of this season's experiences that Davis so nicely sums up his outlook:

"Every day I lead my best life, doesn't matter what I'm doing. I'm just happy to be here. There's not a lot of people in this position, and I'm not supposed to be here. Got to show gratitude and appreciate the little moments

Defensive lineman Jordan Davis is all smiles on the sidelines after getting to play some offense on senior day and score on a 1-yard touchdown run against Charleston Southern. (Curtis Compton/The Atlanta Journal-Constitution)

from waking up to coming here working – even being in front of you guys (the media). It's an honor, no matter what. Every time I put my feet on the ground it's a blessing."

Not supposed to be here? Seriously? There seems to be no one more meant to be a part of this defense-driven team than Davis. He is nothing less than an anchor point. A weight-bearing beam.

Yet, he insists, "Life carries different paths, and I never expected my path to take me here. Every time I'm grateful for it. It almost brings me to tears. I'm not supposed to be here, but I'm here and I'm forever grateful."

Such is the approach of a reformed overweight couch spud and deluded basketball wannabe who had to be practically towed onto the football field as a high schooler in North Carolina. First steps were torture for Davis. As a freshman, he reportedly used to hide in a bathroom stall to try to avoid working out with his high school team. And even after gaining some prep props, his initiation at Georgia hardly was seamless. He was some 40 pounds heavier then, struggling to keep up with the demands. As he once told ESPN, "I was so ready to go back home. I was like, 'Man, I can't do this anymore.'"

Yet through the prodding of teammates and his own day-to-day resolve, the 6-foot-6 Davis began growing into his potential. By late in his freshman season, he had his first start. First an intermittent presence, he gradually became recognized as a larger-than-life figure even in a game filled with mesomorphs. Sloppy fat became more usefully proportioned width. His combination of heft and nimbleness sets him apart, the kind of rare skill set that made Davis an Outland Trophy winner even with the modest stat line (24 tackles, 3.5 for a loss, 2 sacks) and the confinement to the role of early-down specialist.

Even against Alabama, the defending champion and the once standard for all things defense, Davis figures to physically stand above everyone else on that field. You can't help but watch him, drawing all eyes to a position that traditionally goes unnoticed and unloved.

Jordan Davis celebrates after bringing down Missouri wide receiver Dominic Lovett in Georgia's 43-6 win over Missouri. (Hyosub Shin/The Atlanta Journal-Constitution)

Working against an offensive line that gave up seven sacks and 11 tackles for a loss against Auburn, Davis is far more charitable than most when assessing the impending match-up.

"Alabama's always been known for physical toughness, and they have a great offensive line," he said. "They have a great size, great motor. I just feel like it's going to be a tremendous challenge to play against them. They're big. We're big."

No one is bigger than he. And he draws praise to scale. In its entirety, Saban's recent review of Davis' work was a veritable ode.

"I think the guy is one of the most dominant players in college football," the Alabama head coach said. "Any defensive lineman, I guess you can look at a lot of things, but the No. 1 thing is how hard are they to block? And he's really hard to block. He's got great size. He's very powerful, but he's got really good initial quickness – short-area quickness – and can push the pocket and pass rush.

"He's about as good a player as I've seen for a long time as an inside player on any college football team."

Name: Jordan X. Davis. The X is for Xavier.

Image: That of a flesh-and-blood avalanche, so much mass moving with such shocking quickness. Against Clemson, that translated into two tackles for a loss and a sack. Against Alabama-Birmingham, that produced the highlight of the interior lineman running cross-field and running down quarterback Tyler Johnson at the sideline.

Likeness: Yeah, everybody likes Davis. How can you not?

Have no doubt, Davis is supposed to be here. Right in the middle of all good things about this Georgia season. ■

A force to be reckoned with throughout the season, Jordan Davis (99) teams up with Bulldogs linebacker Robert Beal Jr. (33) to stop Florida Gators running back Nay'Quan Wright. (Bob Andres/The Atlanta Journal-Constitution)

ALABAMA 41, GEORGIA 24
December 4, 2021 • Atlanta, Georgia

WAKE-UP CALL

UGA Leads Alabama by 10 – and Loses SEC Championship

By Mark Bradley

Maybe next time, huh? Maybe January 10 in Indianapolis for the national title. Maybe that will – once and forever – be the time Georgia beats Alabama in a game of significance. We thought the moment would come in the SEC Championship game. Yet again, we thought wrong.

Alabama entered the SEC Championship game against No. 1 Georgia as a 6½-point underdog, something the Crimson Tide hadn't been since 2009. As always happens when these teams meet, the Bulldogs built a lead. As always happens when these teams meet, Alabama won. Final score: 41-24.

Said Nick Saban, speaking of us sweethearts in the media: "You gave us a lot of positive rat poison (in noting that Alabama wasn't favored). That rat poison is usually fatal. This rat poison you gave us this week was yummy."

In the grand scheme, losing shouldn't mean much to Georgia. It still will make the College Football Playoff, just not as the No. 1 seed. Thing is, Alabama will make it, too. Georgia hasn't beaten Bama since September 22, 2007, seven meetings ago.

Georgia under Kirby Smart has done everything except win it all and beat Alabama. There seems no way the Bulldogs can manage one without the other, and it's entirely possible that a rematch could favor the Bulldogs. (Why? Who knows? Law of averages, maybe.) But the SEC championship game looked for all the world like Georgia's long-awaited day of deliverance, and it came undone faster than you can count Saban's title-winning rings.

"It didn't do any damage," Smart said of the loss. "What it did was reinvigorate our energy. ... It was a great wake-up call."

For the fourth time in nine years, Georgia built a double-figure lead over Alabama in Atlanta. Given the outcome of those first three games, Smart might have been prudent to ask kicker Jack Podlesny to miss the PAT on purpose. The kick sailed true. Georgia led 10-0 four seconds into the second quarter.

At that moment – this has seemed true of other moments in this series – the Bulldogs looked too good for Bama. George Pickens, back after a torn ACL, outfought safety Jordan Battle for the gain that set up Georgia's first touchdown. The 6-foot-7 tight end Darnell Washington reached above linebacker Henry To'oTo'o to pluck Stetson Bennett's throw from on high to score that touchdown.

Bennett completed eight of his first 10 passes for 126 yards. Georgia outgained the Tide 156 yards to 49 in

Quarterback Stetson Bennett is helped up after getting leveled by Alabama defensive lineman Phidarian Mathis. Despite a strong start by the Bulldogs, Alabama got the best of Georgia for a 41-24 loss. (Curtis Compton/The Atlanta Journal-Constitution)

the game's first 15 minutes and four seconds. The Bulldogs couldn't have scripted a better start. Somehow, though, this movie always ends the same way.

Jameson Williams, Alabama's best receiver, flashed unencumbered down the middle of the field and turned a modest pitch-and-catch into a 67-yard touchdown. It was wretched coverage by any defense. By Georgia's standards, it beggared belief. This 10-point lead was about to go the way of all Georgia leads against Bama.

Asked afterward what he might say to his team if Georgia and Alabama meet in the playoff, Smart said: "The first answer would be, 'Don't leave them uncovered.'"

Then: "We had two or three busts on third down. That's unlike us."

The team that yielded no more than 17 points in a game over 12 games was outscored 24-7 in the second quarter. The Bulldogs entered having yielded 230.9 yards per game. Alabama amassed 316 yards in these 15 minutes. Bryce Young threw for 286 yards and ran for 40 more. He had a hand in all three touchdowns. The nation's best defense managed no sacks in the half, or the game.

Said Smart: "You have to affect the quarterback. You have to get to him and finish. He's so good at avoiding the rush that he buys time to make plays downfield."

A signature moment came when Nakobe Dean, the highly decorated linebacker, bore down on Young and slammed into him as the quarterback threw. A near-sack became a 22-yard completion.

Said Dean: "They've got great players, and they made great plays."

Not two minutes into the third quarter, Bama led 31-17. Williams ran past Lewis Cine and snagged Young's rainbow. Georgia trailed 31-17. It faced its first double-figure deficit since Cincinnati led 21-10 on New Year's Day.

The Bulldogs took their time in responding. Two drives took them beyond the Alabama 20. Neither ended in points. Bennett threw an interception on the first. The second ended on the quarter's final play, a Bennett incompletion

Alabama defensive back DeMarcco Hellams (2) intercepts a pass intended for Georgia tight end Brock Bowers (19). (Hyosub Shin/The Atlanta Journal-Constitution)

on fourth-and-9. (Going for it, as opposed to kicking a field goal that would have left Georgia 11 points behind, was the right choice. It just didn't work.)

Remember when Alabama used to be known for its defense? With Young following in the gilded footsteps of Tua Tagovailoa and Mac Jones and Georgia's defense having surrendered next to nothing all season, nobody gave Bama's defense much of a look in the run-up to this game. On Georgia's first series of the fourth quarter, Bennett threw for Kenny McIntosh, who wasn't open. Battle cut in front and took his interception the distance. It was 38-17 with 11:59 remaining.

For the record, Smart was asked if he might – if this sounds strange, you haven't followed the wayfaring career of Stetson Bennett – consider changing quarterbacks for the playoff. (JT Daniels never moved off the sideline.) Said Smart: "I have the utmost confidence in Stetson Bennett. He did some really nice things today."

Back to the game, or what was left of it. Brock Bowers, the tremendous tight end, scored to bring the Bulldogs within 14. Saban opted not to go for it on fourth-and-1. Enough time remained for Georgia to score two touchdowns, but a false start turned fourth-and-10 into fourth-and-15, which prompted Smart to change his mind and punt. Bama took the ball with 7:08 remaining and began to move – slowly, for once. A field goal with 1:59 left removed all doubt.

Young finished with 421 yards passing against the nation's No. 1 defense. Alabama heads to the playoff for the seventh time in eight years. And Georgia? Well, the Bulldogs do as they've done many times. They pick themselves up and try to imagine some way they can beat Alabama. It has to happen sometime, doesn't it?

Don't answer that. ■

Georgia receiver George Pickens catches a 37-yard pass from Stetson Bennett. Despite the disappointing loss, Kirby Smart reaffirmed his confidence in Bennett heading into the playoff. (Hyosub Shin/The Atlanta Journal-Constitution)

17
LINEBACKER

NAKOBE DEAN

Georgia linebacker Nakobe Dean Wins Butkus Award

By Chip Towers • December 5, 2021

Georgia junior inside linebacker Nakobe Dean was the surprise recipient of the 37th Butkus Award, named after Pro Football Hall of Famer Dick Butkus, and presented annually to the player considered the best linebacker in college football.

Butkus and his son, Matt, surprised Dean with the trophy during a team meeting at Butts-Mehre Heritage Hall in Athens on December 5.

Dean becomes Georgia's second Butkus recipient. He follows Roquan Smith – now of Butkus' Chicago Bears – who won the award in 2017.

Dean received 34% of the weighted vote and 52% of first-place votes, according to the Butkus Award committee's news release. Dean also won the 2018 Butkus Award for high school players as a senior at Horn Lake (Miss.) High.

A 6-foot, 225-pound junior who is majoring in mechanical engineering, Dean started all 13 games during the Bulldogs 2021 season, and 23 in a row dating to the previous season. He had 61 tackles and five quarterback sacks.

"Nakobe Dean is a playmaker with a special combination of strength, coverage ability, playmaking flair and leadership skill," the Butkus committee said in a statement. "He consistently makes his presence felt on the field and in the community, elevates the defense with his command and is a complete linebacker who has made a tremendous impact on Georgia's program."

Finishing second was Devin Lloyd of Utah with 30% of the weighted vote. Others receiving votes were Leo Chenal of Wisconsin (15%), Damone Clark of LSU (7%), Darrian Beavers of Cincinnati (7%), Chad Muma of Wyoming (7%), and DeMarvion Overshown with a write-in vote.

The Butkus selection committee consists of 51 football coaches, recruiters, talent scouts and journalists, who submit a 3-2-1 weighted vote in a confidential ballot. The primary requirements are "toughness, on-field leadership, competitiveness, football character and linebacking skills." ■

Nakobe Dean celebrates after sacking Clemson quarterback DJ Uiagalelei during the first quarter of Georgia's season-opening win over Clemson. In 2021, Dean won the Butkus Award, presented annually to the player considered to be the best linebacker in college football. (Curtis Compton/The Atlanta Journal-Constitution)

Nakobe Dean leaps to stop Kentucky quarterback Will Levis short of the end zone during the Bulldogs' Oct. 16 win in Athens. (Curtis Compton/The Atlanta Journal-Constitution)

19

TIGHT END

BROCK BOWERS

Georgia Freshman Brock Bowers a Coast-to-Coast Hit

By Steve Hummer • December 23, 2021

There wasn't a whole lot in the wispy sports section that DeAnna Bowers had set aside. But what was there was prime. Worth keeping for posterity, really.

The front-page headline in the Napa Valley Register – "Bowers Grabs All-SEC, All-America Honors" – called out in a rather loud and excited font.

Newspapers may shrink, but the stories they tell thankfully don't.

Bold type has broken out all around Georgia freshman tight end Brock Bowers. Yet his family, some 2,500 miles west of Athens at the gateway to northern California wine country, still grapples with the message. Wonder mixed with disbelief makes for a superb, heady blend that pairs well with football.

"You look at that," DeAnna said, nodding to the paper, "and say, somebody's kid is doing really well.

"Then you have to remind yourself, 'Wait, that's our kid.'"

Certainly, Bowers has been a revelation for Georgia fans. From the opening game at Clemson when he had a team-leading six receptions. To the most recent contest against Alabama, when he was the best thing the Bulldogs had going in a loss, setting an SEC Championship game record with 10 catches.

Bowers had come from outside the comfort zone of the Southern football following, from a place rich in clichés and misunderstandings about cabernet and brie and a general casual attitude about a game that we in the right-hand corner of the country know to be as important as water, air and a hip flask on Saturday. These people do realize you get after football, hard, right from kickoff, that you don't uncork it and let it breathe, right?

Little could we know that when Bowers enrolled early in 2021, the Bulldogs had in the fold just another pickup-driving, hunt-anything-that-moves good ol' boy who loves him some 'ball.

How much does he love it? Well, his mother thought Brock might have broken the kitchen counter after he heard about the state of California canceling his senior season at Napa High because of COVID-19, so fiercely did he slam his fist in frustration.

Bowers' relationship with the sport is obvious to those of Georgia persuasion now. Finishing the 2021 season with a team-leading 791 receiving yards, with 11 of his 47 catches for touchdowns, Bowers got himself named SEC Freshman of the Year and placed on

Brock Bowers led the Bulldogs with 10 catches for 139 yards against the Crimson Tide, setting a record for tight ends in the SEC Championship game. (Hyosub Shin/The Atlanta Journal-Constitution)

various All-American and All-SEC teams. And forever will his name be linked to the vision of a 6-foot-4, 230-pound tight end running down the middle of the field at Georgia Tech, Yellow Jackets defensive backs seeming to have an angle on him, yet still losing ground on every step toward the end zone.

Just as Bulldogs fans had much to learn about Bowers – and they had to do it without the benefit of hearing from him, given Kirby Smart's interview blackout of all freshmen – so did his people. These were not the kind of parents filled with delusions that their child was born for Canton, Ohio. Warren and DeAnna met at Utah State, where he was a center on the football team and she a pitcher and first baseman on the softball squad. They have a practical, firsthand relationship with athletic ability. And that meant they had questions before their boy left wine country for the faraway SEC.

How would Brock handle the jump from a middling high school program – one that went dark his senior year, and one that had been sapped by a hazing scandal just as he was entering ninth grade – to a college program with national championship aspirations?

His had been a completely immersive northern California upbringing. Why, there's a giant redwood not 50 yards from his front door. How would Bowers acclimate to such a foreign setting as Georgia?

Was he really good enough?

"I'm thinking he's going to an SEC school, all right, maybe he's running down on a couple kickoffs. Maybe he's on special teams," said his father, Warren.

The answers all have come back positive. Still, there's a cautious attitude at work that seems to have served Brock well. No one conceded anything. Nothing was taken for granted nor deemed an entitlement. And that still plays well today.

Said Nathan Kenion, the local trainer who began working with Brock in the eighth grade and pushed him out on the national 7-on-7 circuit: "Why I gravitated toward Brock and his parents is they were never like, our son is the greatest. Warren was like, 'I know my son is

good in Napa, but this is Napa.' He was always kind of blown away how his son played outside of the realm of where he was from."

Brock certainly had the gene pool working for him – as did his sister, a collegiate softball player. One of his parents is even in their college's athletic hall of fame.

"That's not a good topic," DeAnna said, laughing.

"It's relatively irritating because it gets brought up a lot," Warren added. "Everyone thinks someone brought everything to the table, and it wasn't me. I'm reminded of that a lot, by a lot of people."

So, you get the idea which one here is in the Utah State Hall? And maybe who takes credit for passing along the kind of eyebrow-arching speed Bowers showed in the Tech game?

The kid always had the innate competitiveness needed to thrive on the field. As a 5-year-old soccer player he once had to be pulled from a game after running himself to the point of near breathless collapse trying to chase down a kid who took the ball from him. Playing both ways at Napa High – in fact, Notre Dame initially offered him as a linebacker – you practically needed a court order to get him out of the game. That reminded his mother of the night she considered calling 9-1-1 after one game when her exhausted son was locked up in cramps on the living room floor.

It was Kenion who offered the Bowers family an initial hint of what could be possible for Brock. When he first met Brock as an eighth grader at a tryout for the 7-on-7 program, Kenion took one look at the tall, slight, curly-haired specimen before him and wondered, "Is this kid a swimmer?" Then he saw Brock run – smooth, uncommonly graceful and fast – and the angels sang.

Kenion was high on Brock then: "In eighth grade I told his dad he's going to be one of the top recruits in the nation by the time his turn comes."

And even higher on him now: "I've compared him to Kelce (Kansas City's Travis) – and I still think he's a little different than him."

The premonition of intense recruitment came true.

Brock Bowers scored two touchdowns during Georgia's 45-0 win over Georgia Tech on November 27. (Hyosub Shin/The Atlanta Journal-Constitution)

No matter the distance, the Bulldogs were on Brock early – it became something of a joke among DeAnna's math students at Napa every time Georgia tight end coach Todd Hartley showed up to visit. "Oh, here's Georgia again," they'd say.

As Brock looked around the big wide world of college sport, he knew what he didn't like. Big-city schools such as Washington, USC, UCLA were out. He is small-town at heart and prefers the open spaces of a pond and a duck blind in hunting season, a pursuit his father fostered. Some programs slept on him. Others didn't come up with the game-plan goods, not showing a willingness to deploy him all over the field as Georgia has – in tight, in the slot or out wide.

His coach at Napa, a former Penn State defensive back, had hoped his guy would end up in Happy Valley. Alas, said Askari Adams, "I remember when he came back from visiting Georgia, he just loved it out there. Georgia checked almost every danged box he was looking at – the hunting, the good football, that atmosphere, the country life."

"(Brock) was like, I can't stay out West; it's just not the same," his father said. "He wanted to play on the biggest stage."

"We don't do football like that, it's just different out here," his mom added. "He wanted the Dawg Walk. He wanted that tradition, and he told me he wanted to compete with the best people."

The life of a bicoastal football family isn't easy. Warren, a partner in a construction firm, and DeAnna, a teacher on sabbatical, made the commitment of at least one of them being at every Georgia game. She estimates she's made 15 cross-country round trips this year and Warren just a handful fewer.

When recruiters called Kenion, he'd tell every one of them that if you sign Brock, you're getting a gift. "He's everything you're looking at on paper – and then you're not getting the prima donna or the attitude." (Here's commitment: His mother tells of Brock turning down a relatively low-paying Name, Image, Likeness gig with Tom Brady's clothing line because it would interfere with his game-week prep).

Such a big noise Brock is making at Georgia that they're hearing it all the way out in California wine country. On Mondays after a Bulldogs game, Adams found his kids at Napa High going over highlights. His parents now hear from friends and neighbors who before probably thought SEC stood only for Securities and Exchange Commission, but now talk like they're related to Vince Dooley. The crew at Fire Station House No. 5 in Napa has gone as far as to borrow a Georgia "G" flag from the Bowers family and pin it up in their weight room.

You want a truly disorienting experience, get off a phone call with Napa Fire Captain Joey Oliva and have him sign off with a, "Go Dawgs."

Brock has inspired plenty of glad wonderment throughout Georgia's traditional range. That now extends to the Napa Valley as well. Seems they do raise more than sommeliers in these parts.

Said Adams, the high school coach, "I'm not going to sit here and say I knew he could do this. Did I think he could be competitive and do well? Yeah. But I never imagined him exploding this early and doing so well because it is the SEC. For a true freshman to come out and do the things he's doing, I never saw that coming. Damn, right from the first game."

His father remembers a lot of conversations with Brock that followed the themes of staying humble and keeping in mind there's always somebody out there who just might be better. "I kind of downplayed that he was any good, to tell you the truth. Because I didn't know how good he was," Warren said.

"We had no idea it would be like this," he said. "It's overwhelming." ∎

Brock Bowers stretches for a long first down during Georgia's win over Florida on October 20. (Bob Andres/The Atlanta Journal-Constitution)

ORANGE BOWL

GEORGIA 34, MICHIGAN 11

December 31, 2021 • Miami Gardens, Florida

THE ROAD TO REDEMPTION

Bulldogs Manhandle Michigan to Gain Alabama Rematch

By Chip Towers

After the game clock had finally ticked down to double zeroes at Hard Rock Stadium and Georgia's 34-11 win over Michigan was official, Kirby Smart's players sought to give him a Gatorade bath.

The Bulldogs' coach was having none of it. He avoided the dunk and scolded those that tried to give it to him.

"I was wanting a real shower and not a Gatorade bath," Smart explained after the College Football Playoff semifinal victory. "Because I want to get focused on Alabama. They have a five- or six-hour head start. To be honest, I'm not interested in celebrating that. We'll look back on that win, and that'll be great. But we're focused on the task ahead."

That'd be another matchup with Alabama (13-1) in the national championship. The No. 1-ranked Crimson Tide defeated No. 4 Cincinnati 27-6 in the Cotton Bowl in Arlington, Texas.

The Bulldogs (13-1) played the Tide in the CFP finals Jan. 8, 2018, at Mercedes-Benz Stadium and lost 26-23 in overtime. Georgia also lost to Bama 41-24 in the SEC Championship game at the Benz on Dec. 4.

Now the burgeoning SEC rivals will meet again Jan. 10 in the 2021 CFP Championship game at Lucas Oil Stadium in Indianapolis.

For Georgia, it could represent The Great Do Over or the football equivalent of beating one's head against a wall. The Bulldogs have lost their past seven games against Alabama.

As dominant as the Michigan win before 66,839 spectators was, it had to be particularly satisfying for Georgia's senior quarterback Stetson Bennett. He was named the Orange Bowl's offensive MVP after passing for 310 yards and three touchdowns with no interceptions and nary a misstep.

"This game is all about how well you play," said Bennett, a fifth-year senior and former walk-on from Blackshear. "I didn't go out there and play well today in spite of people. I came out there and played hard and worked hard throughout the last few weeks because my teammates needed me to do that and we needed to win.

The No. 3 Bulldogs (13-1) won a College Football Playoff semifinal for the second time under Smart and improved to 2-1 all-time against Michigan (12-2), which came in as the Big Ten champion.

Quarterback Stetson Bennett tosses oranges to teammates after Georgia's 34-11 win over Michigan in the Orange Bowl. Bennett was named the game's offensive MVP after passing for 310 yards and three touchdowns. (Curtis Compton/The Atlanta Journal-Constitution)

Georgia senior cornerback Derion Kendrick was named the Orange Bowl's outstanding defensive player. A Clemson transfer who twice played in the playoff before joining the Bulldogs, Kendrick had two interceptions and finished with five tackles, including a tackle for loss.

Kendrick also had a tough outing the last time out against Alabama, which threw for more than 400 yards against Georgia.

"As a football player, you're always ready to go out there regardless of what game it is," Kendrick said. "We're ready to go regardless who the opponent is. It just so happens it's Alabama who beat us. We've got to go back and clean up some things we did."

The Orange Bowl was decided fairly early for the Bulldogs. They jumped on Michigan quickly, scoring touchdowns on their first two possessions of the game and on five of their first six before the first-half clock ran out on them at midfield.

At that point, Bennett had completed 16 of 22 passes for 234 yards and two touchdowns. His scoring tosses went to Jermaine Burton for 57 yards and to Brock Bowers for nine yards, and he had 53- and 35-yard completions in the opening half. Bennett added a key run in the first quarter in which he evaded the pressure of Heisman Trophy finalist Aidan Hutchinson from the left and for a 20-yard gain.

Bennett's most satisfying moment may have come at the 11:11 mark of the game. That's when he hit James Cook with his third touchdown pass of the game, a 39-yarder that put the score out of reach at 34-3. It also put Bennett over 300 yards for the game.

"I mean, as a leader, Stetson doesn't let all that negativity go to his head. For real," Cook said. "He ain't got no social media. He carries a flip phone around and he just lets the noise go over his head and plays football. That's what I love about him."

It was a pretty good night for Cook as well. A senior running back who grew up seven miles south of Hard Rock Stadium, Cook had 99 yards receiving and 131 total yards on the night.

Derion Kendrick holds up the Orange Bowl trophy as he and his teammates celebrate following the win over Michigan. With the win, Georgia moved on to play Alabama for the national championship. (Hyosub Shin/The Atlanta Journal-Constitution)

"My mom, my aunties, my cousins, my stepdad, my girlfriend, my brother – not Dalvin (of the Minnesota Vikings) because he's got a game – they were all here supporting me tonight," Cook said. "I'm just happy we're going to be playing another game, just getting another win. I wasn't going to be satisfied unless we did."

Meanwhile, Michigan, one of the best pass-rushing teams in the country, finished with zero sacks.

"Got to give them credit," Wolverines coach Jim Harbaugh said. "They executed well. Game plan was good and we weren't able to keep pace."

Leading 27-3 at halftime, the Bulldogs avoided Michigan's biggest bullet on the Wolverines' first possession of the third quarter. Kendrick picked up his second interception of the game when he picked off Michigan's Cade McNamara in the Georgia end zone at the 9:57 mark. That would be the Wolverines' last meaningful threat.

It was another great night for Georgia's defense, which was left with some doubts with the loss to Alabama four weeks prior. The Bulldogs stopped Michigan short on fourth-and-goal from their 6 with seven minutes to play. It was the third time on the night that Georgia's offense was able to take over on downs.

Averaging 452 yards and 37.7 points per game, the Wolverines had 290 yards and three points, respectively, when Georgia sent its starting defenders to the sideline. Almost immediately, Michigan scored its first touchdown of the game on a 35-yard TD pass to Andrei Anthony with 4:25 to play. The Wolverines got a 2-point conversion as well to make the score 34-11.

The Wolverines, who came out on the field before the game in shirts inscribed with "run the damn ball," were limited to 88 yards on the ground.

"There was a little chip on the shoulders of our defensive guys," Smart said. "Their offensive coordinator got the Broyles Award over coach (Dan) Lanning, who we think did one hell of a job. Their offensive line got the Joe Moore Award. ... But we've got one hell of an offensive line, too."

Derion Kendrick intercepts a pass in the end zone during the third quarter. Kendrick was named the Orange Bowl's outstanding defensive player after finishing with two interceptions and five tackles. (Hyosub Shin/The Atlanta Journal-Constitution)

Georgia's win ties the school record for wins in a season. The Bulldogs also had 13 victories in 2017 (13-2) and 2002.

It was the fourth Orange Bowl appearance for Georgia and the third match-up in history with Michigan. The Bulldogs are now 2-1 against the Wolverines, playing them for the first time since 1965. They're now 3-1 in the Orange Bowl, with the last win coming against Missouri in 1960 (14-0).

In their other CFP appearance, the Bulldogs' defeated No. 2-ranked Oklahoma 54-48 in double overtime of the 2017 Rose Bowl. Georgia lost to Alabama a week later in the national championship game at Mercedes-Benz Stadium, also in overtime, 26-23.

Michigan was making its first appearance in the playoffs. The Wolverines (12-2) won their first Big Ten championship since 2004 in 2021.

Smart and Harbaugh both were attempting to become the first coaches since Tennessee's Phillip Fulmer in 1998 to win a national champion for their alma mater. Only Smart still has that opportunity. ■

Opposite: Stetson Bennett runs away from Michigan defensive lineman Julius Welschof for a gain during the second quarter. Above: Offensive lineman Justin Shaffer (right) hoists running back James Cook after Cook's touchdown in the fourth quarter of the Orange Bowl. (Hyosub Shin/The Atlanta Journal-Constitution)

Epilogue

By Brandon Adams

As I watched this magical season unfold for Georgia along the way to winning its first national championship in more than 40 years, there was one thought that repeatedly entered my head: What would Larry Munson have to say about all this?

Munson was, of course, the legendary former play-by-play broadcaster for UGA games on the radio, and his calls of the most memorable moments from the Bulldogs' last championship season in 1980 are as much a part of the program's lore as any of the coaches or players.

I am old enough to have been alive back then, but not old enough to have any memories of it. Instead, my memories as a lifelong UGA fan are about how I learned of that era by listening to the pivotal plays from that season as narrated by Munson on audio tapes.

The thing that jumped out at me about those recordings was the way Munson made fans feel as if they were a part of the team. He did this by saying "we" a lot.

For instance, when UGA beat Florida in 1980 on the famous Lindsay Scott touchdown catch that propelled the Bulldogs to a come-from-behind victory and helped preserve an unbeaten season, Munson summed up the miraculous nature of the moment in a way only he could.

"We were gone," Munson said at the time. "I gave up. You did too. We were out of it and gone."

Using the word "we" as frequently as Munson did – as if he were on the team – is the kind of thing young broadcasters are taught not to do. Yet, ignoring the best practices of broadcast schools is one of the things that made Munson so endearing.

In other words, it may not have been technically correct, but it still felt right.

And all these decades later, the connection between team and fan that Munson conjured up still feels right to many of us.

Bulldogs fans might not ever catch a pass or make a tackle, but they have undoubtedly played a crucial role in bringing a national championship back to UGA.

Seeing tens of thousands of red-and-black-clad partisans in the stands of the game – no matter how far Georgia might be from home – has become commonplace, including this year's College Football Playoff games in Miami and Indianapolis.

UGA coach Kirby Smart has frequently credited those fans for creating the kind of atmosphere that has helped the Bulldogs win.

Plus, many of those same fans have proven to be generous donors as well – giving the kind of money to their beloved program that's allowed it to continuously upgrade facilities and maintain a competitive edge.

In fact, it can be argued that UGA had a championship-level fan base well before it fielded a team that could match it.

However, the real connection forged around Georgia football is about much more than making a contribution to the team's success.

The audio tapes that made me first appreciate Munson – and helped me learn about the Bulldogs' history – were given to me by my father. And he told me tales of the exploits of Herschel Walker, the subject of so many great Munson calls, the way his father had told him about the best player from his generation, Charley Trippi.

Now, through the good times and the bad, I get to share my love of the Bulldogs with my own children.

When people refer to UGA as "we," that's often

Larry Munson was the voice of Georgia football from 1966 to 2008. He passed away in 2011 at the age of 89. (Curtis Compton/The Atlanta Journal-Constitution)

what they mean. It's not just them and the team; it's them and all those they've shared the joy of fandom with through the years.

Because as much as I would love to know what Munson would think about these Dawgs, what I really wish I knew is what my dad would think about them. Unfortunately, he passed away last year.

As anyone who has experienced a loss can tell you, the memories of a loved one become priceless once that person is no longer with us. My memories of my father are about Georgia football – of attending games together when I was a child, of listening to old Munson tapes and dreaming of when the Bulldogs might have

another championship season to celebrate.

In other words, my dad is a part of my "we," and I hope my children think of me that way when they give the gift of being a fan to their own children.

I also hope they don't have to wait another 40 years to experience the Bulldogs' next national championship. But even if they do, their lives will be no less rich – because the relationships they build around their favorite team are more valuable than a trophy.

That's what I'll think about when I think of Georgia football in 2021. It was the year we finally did it. We won the national championship – all of us, including the ones who are no longer with us. ∎

Quarterback Stetson Bennett thanks fans as he leaves the field at Hard Rock Stadium following the Orange Bowl. (Hyosub Shin/The Atlanta Journal-Constitution)